Fortinet Network Security Expert 5 (NSE5) Exam Practice Questions & Dumps

Exam Practice Questions for Fortinet
NSE5
LATEST VERSION

Presented by: Quantic Books

About Quantic Books:

Quantic Books is a publishing house based in Princeton, New Jersey, USA. , a platform that is accessible online as well as locally, which gives power to educational content, erudite collection, poetry & many other book genres. We make it easy for writers & authors to get their books designed, published, promoted, and sell professionally on worldwide scale with eBook + Print distribution. Quantic Books is now distributing books worldwide.

Note: Find answers of the questions at the last of the book.

QUESTION 1

Which statement is correct regarding virus scanning on a FortiGate unit?

A. Virus scanning is enabled by default.
B. Fortinet Customer Support enables virus scanning remotely for you.
C. Virus scanning must be enabled in a UTM security profile and the UTM security profile must be assigned to a firewall policy.
D. Enabling virus scanning in a UTM security profile enables virus scanning for all traffic flowing through the FortiGate device.

QUESTION 2

Which of the following statements are correct regarding URL filtering on the FortiGate unit? (Select all that apply.)

A. The allowed actions for URL Filtering include Allow, Block and Exempt.
B. The allowed actions for URL Filtering are Allow and Block.
C. The FortiGate unit can filter URLs based on patterns using text and regular expressions.
D. Any URL accessible by a web browser can be blocked using URL Filtering.
E. Multiple URL Filter lists can be added to a single protection profile.

QUESTION 3

Which of the following regular expression patterns will make the terms "confidential data" case insensitive?

A. \[confidential data]
B. /confidential data/i
C. i/confidential data/
D. "confidential data"
E. /confidential data/c

QUESTION 4

Which of the following spam filtering methods are supported on the FortiGate unit? (Select all that apply.)

A. IP Address Check
B. Open Relay Database List (ORDBL)
C. Black/White List
D. Return Email DNS Check
E. Email Checksum Check

QUESTION 5

Which of the following email spam filtering features is NOT supported on a FortiGate unit?

A. Multipurpose Internet Mail Extensions (MIME) Header Check
B. HELO DNS Lookup
C. Greylisting
D. Banned Word

QUESTION 6

Examine the exhibit shown below; then answer the question following it.

Which of the following statements best describes the green status indicators that appear next to the different FortiGuard Distribution Network services as illustrated in the exhibit?

FortiGuard Subscription Services

AntiVirus	Valid License (Expires 2013-05-12)	✅
AV Definitions	1.00000 (Updated 2012-10-17 *via Manual Update*) [Update]	
AV Engine	5.00032 (Updated 2012-10-16 *via Manual Update*)	
IPS	Valid License (Expires 2013-05-12)	✅
IPS Definitions	4.00269 (Updated 2012-11-28 *via Manual Update*) [Update]	
IPS Engine	2.00043 (Updated 2012-10-29 *via Manual Update*)	
Vulnerability Scan	Valid License (Expires 2013-05-12)	✅
VCM Plugins	1.00288 (Updated 2012-11-30 *via Manual Update*) [Update]	
VCM Engine	1.00288 (Updated 2012-11-30 *via Manual Update*)	
Web Filtering	Valid License (Expires 2013-05-11)	✅
Email Filtering	Valid License (Expires 2013-05-11)	✅

A. They indicate that the FortiGate unit is able to connect to the FortiGuard Distribution Network.

B. They indicate that the FortiGate unit has the latest updates that are available from the FortiGuard Distribution Network.

C. They indicate that updates are available and should be downloaded from the FortiGuard Distribution Network to the FortiGate unit.

D. They indicate that the FortiGate unit is in the process of downloading updates from the FortiGuard Distribution Network.

QUESTION 7

A FortiGate unit is configured to receive push updates from the FortiGuard Distribution Network, however, updates are not being received. Which of the following statements are possible reasons for this? (Select all that apply.)

A. The external facing interface of the FortiGate unit is configured to use DHCP.
B. The FortiGate unit has not been registered.
C. There is a NAT device between the FortiGate unit and the FortiGuard Distribution Network and no override push IP is configured.
D. The FortiGate unit is in Transparent mode which does not support push updates.

QUESTION 8

Which of the following statements best describes the proxy behavior on a FortiGate unit during an FTP client upload when FTP splice is disabled?

A. The proxy will not allow a file to be transmitted in multiple streams simultaneously.
B. The proxy sends the file to the server while simultaneously buffering it.
C. If the file being scanned is determined to be infected, the proxy deletes it from the server by sending a delete command on behalf of the client.
D. If the file being scanned is determined to be clean, the proxy terminates the connection and leaves the file on the server.

QUESTION 9

A firewall policy has been configured for the internal email server to receive email from external parties through SMTP. Exhibits A and B show the antivirus and email filter profiles applied to this policy.

Exhibit A:

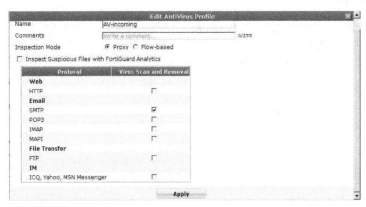

Exhibit B:

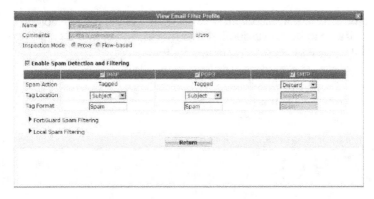

What is the correct behavior when the email attachment is detected as a virus by the FortiGate antivirus engine?

A. The FortiGate unit will remove the infected file and deliver the email with a replacement message to alert the recipient that the original attachment was infected.
B. The FortiGate unit will reject the infected email and the sender will receive a failed delivery message.

C. The FortiGate unit will remove the infected file and add a replacement message. Both sender and recipient are notified that the infected file has been removed.

D. The FortiGate unit will reject the infected email and notify the sender.

QUESTION 10

What are the valid sub-types for a Firewall type policy? (Select all that apply)

A. Device Identity
B. Address
C. User Identity
D. Schedule
E. SSL VPN

QUESTION 11

In NAT/Route mode when there is no matching firewall policy for traffic to be forwarded by the Firewall, which of the following statements describes the action taken on traffic?

A. The traffic is blocked.
B. The traffic is passed.
C. The traffic is passed and logged.
D. The traffic is blocked and logged.

QUESTION 12

In which order are firewall policies processed on the FortiGate unit?

A. They are processed from the top down according to their sequence number.
B. They are processed based on the policy ID number shown in the left hand column of the policy window.
C. They are processed on best match.
D. They are processed based on a priority value assigned through the priority column in the policy window.

QUESTION 13

Which of the following pieces of information can be included in the Destination Address field of a firewall policy? (Select all that apply.)

A. An IP address pool.
B. A virtual IP address.
C. An actual IP address or an IP address group.
D. An FQDN or Geographic value(s).

QUESTION 14

The ordering of firewall policies is very important. Policies can be re-ordered within the FortiGate unit's GUI and also using the CLI. The command used in the CLI to perform this function is_
_____.

A. set order
B. edit policy
C. reorder
D. move

QUESTION 15

You wish to create a firewall policy that applies only to traffic intended for your web server. The web server has an IP address of 192.168.2.2 and a /24 subnet mask. When defining the firewall address for use in this policy, which one of the following addresses is correct?

A. 192.168.2.0 / 255.255.255.0
B. 192.168.2.2 / 255.255.255.0
C. 192.168.2.0 / 255.255.255.255
D. 192.168.2.2 / 255.255.255.255

QUESTION 16

What is the effect of using CLI "config system session-ttl" to set session_ttl to 1800 seconds?

A. Sessions can be idle for no more than 1800 seconds.
B. The maximum length of time a session can be open is 1800 seconds.
C. After 1800 seconds, the end user must reauthenticate.
D. After a session has been open for 1800 seconds, the FortiGate unit will send a keep alive packet to both client and server.

QUESTION 17

Which of the following network protocols are supported for administrative access to a FortiGate unit?

A. HTTPS, HTTP, SSH, TELNET, PING, SNMP
B. FTP, HTTPS, NNTP, TCP, WINS
C. HTTP, NNTP, SMTP, DHCP
D. Telnet, FTP, RLOGIN, HTTP, HTTPS, DDNS
E. Telnet, UDP, NNTP, SMTP

QUESTION 18

Which of the following statements is correct regarding a FortiGate unit operating in NAT/Route mode?

A. The FortiGate unit applies NAT to all traffic.
B. The FortiGate unit functions as a Layer 3 device.
C. The FortiGate unit functions as a Layer 2 device.
D. The FortiGate unit functions as a router and the firewall function is disabled.

QUESTION 19

A FortiGate unit can provide which of the following capabilities? (Select all that apply.)

A. Email filtering
B. Firewall
C. VPN gateway
D. Mail relay
E. Mail server

QUESTION 20

Which of the following methods can be used to access the CLI? (Select all that apply.)

A. By using a direct connection to a serial console.
B. By using the CLI console window in the GUI.
C. By using an SSH connection.
D. By using a Telnet connection.

QUESTION 21

When backing up the configuration file on a FortiGate unit, the contents can be encrypted by enabling the encrypt option and supplying a password. If the password is forgotten, the configuration file can still be restored using which of the following methods?

A. Selecting the recover password option during the restore process.
B. Having the password emailed to the administrative user by selecting the Forgot Password option.
C. Sending the configuration file to Fortinet Support for decryption.
D. If the password is forgotten, there is no way to use the file.

QUESTION 22

When creating administrative users which of the following configuration objects determines access rights on the FortiGate unit.

A. profile
B. allow access interface settings
C. operation mode
D. local-in policy

QUESTION 23

What is the FortiGate unit password recovery process?

A. Interrupt boot sequence, modify the boot registry and reboot. After changing the password, reset the boot registry.
B. Log in through the console port using the "maintainer" account within approximately 30 seconds of a reboot.
C. Hold down the CTRL + Esc (Escape) keys during reboot, then reset the admin password.
D. The only way to regain access is to interrupt the boot sequence and restore a configuration file for which the password has been modified.

QUESTION 24

Which of the following statements are true of the FortiGate unit's factory default configuration?

A. 'Port1' or 'Internal' interface will have an IP of 192.168.1.99.
B. 'Port1' or 'Internal' interface will have a DHCP server set up and enabled (on devices that support DHCP Servers).
C. Default login will always be the username: admin (all lowercase) and no password.
D. The implicit firewall action is ACCEPT.

QUESTION 25

Which of the following are valid FortiGate device interface methods for handling DNS requests? (Select all that apply.)

A. Forward-only
B. Non-recursive
C. Recursive
D. Iterative
E. Conditional-forward

QUESTION 26

The default administrator profile that is assigned to the default "admin" user on a FortGate device is:_____.

A. trusted-admin
B. super_admin
C. super_user
D. admin
E. fortinet-root

QUESTION 27

Which of the following logging options are supported on a FortiGate unit? (Select all that apply.)

A. LDAP
B. Syslog
C. FortiAnalyzer
D. Local disk and/or memory

QUESTION 28

In order to match an identity-based policy, the FortiGate unit checks the IP information. Once inside the policy, the following logic is followed:

A. First, a check is performed to determine if the user's login credentials are valid. Next, the user is checked to determine if they belong to any of the groups defined for that policy. Finally, user restrictions are determined and port, time, and UTM profiles are applied.
B. First, user restrictions are determined and port, time, and UTM profiles are applied. Next, a check is performed to determine if the user's login credentials are valid. Finally, the user is checked to determine if they belong to any of the groups defined for that policy.
C. First, the user is checked to determine if they belong to any of the groups defined for that policy. Next, user restrictions are determined and port, time, and UTM profiles are applied. Finally, a check is performed to determine if the user's login credentials are valid.

QUESTION 29

Which of the following statements regarding the firewall policy authentication timeout is true?

A. The authentication timeout is an idle timeout. This means that the FortiGate unit will consider a user to be "idle" if it does not see any packets coming from the user's source IP.

B. The authentication timeout is a hard timeout. This means that the FortiGate unit will remove the temporary policy for this user's source IP after this timer has expired.

C. The authentication timeout is an idle timeout. This means that the FortiGate unit will consider a user to be "idle" if it does not see any packets coming from the user's source MAC.

D. The authentication timeout is a hard timeout. This means that the FortiGate unit will remove the temporary policy for this user's source MAC after this timer has expired.

QUESTION 30

Two-factor authentication is supported using the following methods? (Select all that apply.)

A. FortiToken
B. Email
C. SMS phone message
D. Code books

QUESTION 31

Which of the following statements are true regarding Local User Authentication? (Select all that apply.)

A. Local user authentication is based on usernames and passwords stored locally on the FortiGate unit.
B. Two-factor authentication can be enabled on a per user basis.
C. Administrators can create an account for the user locally and specify the remote server to verify the password.
D. Local users are for administration accounts only and cannot be used for identity policies.

QUESTION 32

Which of the statements below are true regarding firewall policy disclaimers? (Select all that apply.)

A. User must accept the disclaimer to proceed with the authentication process.
B. The disclaimer page is customizable.
C. The disclaimer cannot be used in combination with user authentication.
D. The disclaimer can only be applied to wireless interfaces.

QUESTION 33

Examine the firewall configuration shown below; then answer the question following it.

Which of the following statements are correct based on the firewall configuration illustrated in the exhibit? (Select all that apply.)

A. A user can access the Internet using only the protocols that are supported by user authentication.

B. A user can access the Internet using any protocol except HTTP, HTTPS, Telnet, and FTP. These require authentication before the user will be allowed access.

C. A user must authenticate using the HTTP, HTTPS, SSH, FTP, or Telnet protocol before they can access any services.

D. A user cannot access the Internet using any protocols unless the user has passed firewall authentication.

QUESTION 34

When browsing to an internal web server using a web-mode SSL VPN bookmark, from which of the following source IP addresses would the web server consider the HTTP request to be initiated?

A. The remote user's virtual IP address.

B. The FortiGate unit's internal IP address.

C. The remote user's public IP address.

D. The FortiGate unit's external IP address.

QUESTION 35

An issue could potentially occur when clicking Connect to start tunnel mode SSL VPN. The tunnel will start up for a few seconds, then shut down. Which of the following statements best describes how to resolve this issue?

A. This user does not have permission to enable tunnel mode. Make sure that the tunnel mode widget has been added to that user's web portal.
B. This FortiGate unit may have multiple Internet connections. To avoid this problem, use the appropriate CLI command to bind the SSL VPN connection to the original incoming interface.
C. Check the SSL adaptor on the host machine. If necessary, uninstall and reinstall the adaptor from the tunnel mode portal.
D. Make sure that only Internet Explorer is used. All other browsers are unsupported.

QUESTION 36

You are the administrator in charge of a FortiGate unit which acts as a VPN gateway. You have chosen to use Interface Mode when configuring the VPN tunnel and you want users from either side to be able to initiate new sessions. There is only 1 subnet at either end and the FortiGate unit already has a default route.

Which of the following configuration steps are required to achieve these objectives? (Select all that apply.)

A. Create one firewall policy.
B. Create two firewall policies.
C. Add a route for the remote subnet.
D. Add a route for incoming traffic.
E. Create a phase 1 definition.
F. Create a phase 2 definition.

QUESTION 37

Which of the following items is NOT a packet characteristic matched by a firewall service object?

A. ICMP type and code
B. TCP/UDP source and destination ports
C. IP protocol number
D. TCP sequence number

QUESTION 38

A firewall policy has been configured such that traffic logging is disabled and a UTM function is enabled.
In addition, the system setting 'utm-incident-traffic-log' has been enabled. In which log will a UTM event message be stored?

A. Traffic
B. UTM
C. System
D. None

QUESTION 39

Which one of the following statements is correct about raw log messages?

A. Logs have a header and a body section. The header will have the same layout for every log message. The body section will change layout from one type of log message to another.
B. Logs have a header and a body section. The header and body will change layout from one type of log message to another.
C. Logs have a header and a body section. The header and body will have the same layout for every log message.

QUESTION 40

Which of the following is an advantage of using SNMP v3 instead of SNMP v1/v2 when querying the FortiGate unit?

A. Packet encryption
B. MIB-based report uploads
C. SNMP access limits through access lists
D. Running SNMP service on a non-standard port is possible

QUESTION 41

Which of the following authentication types are supported by FortiGate units? (Select all that apply.)

A. Kerberos
B. LDAP
C. RADIUS
D. Local Users

QUESTION 42

Which of the following are valid authentication user group types on a FortiGate unit? (Select all that apply.)

A. Firewall
B. Directory Service
C. Local
D. LDAP
E. PKI

QUESTION 43

Users may require access to a web site that is blocked by a policy. Administrators can give users the ability to override the block. Which of the following statements regarding overrides are correct? (Select all that apply.)

A. A protection profile may have only one user group defined as an override group.

B. A firewall user group can be used to provide override privileges for FortiGuard Web Filtering.

C. Authentication to allow the override is based on a user's membership in a user group.

D. Overrides can be allowed by the administrator for a specific period of time.

QUESTION 44

Users may require access to a web site that is blocked by a policy. Administrators can give users the ability to override the block. Which of the following statements regarding overrides is NOT correct?

A. A web filter profile may only have one user group defined as an override group.

B. A firewall user group can be used to provide override privileges for FortiGuard Web Filtering.

C. When requesting an override, the matched user must belong to a user group for which the override capabilty has been enabled.

D. Overrides can be allowed by the administrator for a specific period of time.

QUESTION 45

An administrator has configured a FortiGate unit so that end users must authenticate against the firewall using digital certificates before browsing the Internet. What must the user have for a successful authentication? (Select all that apply.)

A. An entry in a supported LDAP Directory.
B. A digital certificate issued by any CA server.
C. A valid username and password.
D. A digital certificate issued by the FortiGate unit.
E. Membership in a firewall user group.

QUESTION 46

The FortiGate unit can be configured to allow authentication to a RADIUS server. The RADIUS server can use several different authentication protocols during the authentication process. Which of the following are valid authentication protocols that can be used when a user authenticates to the RADIUS server? (Select all that apply.)

A. MS-CHAP-V2 (Microsoft Challenge-Handshake Authentication Protocol v2)
B. PAP (Password Authentication Protocol)
C. CHAP (Challenge-Handshake Authentication Protocol)
D. MS-CHAP (Microsoft Challenge-Handshake Authentication Protocol v1)
E. FAP (FortiGate Authentication Protocol)

QUESTION 47

Which of the following are valid components of the Fortinet Server Authentication Extensions (FSAE)? (Select all that apply.)

A. Domain Local Security Agent.
B. Collector Agent.
C. Active Directory Agent.
D. User Authentication Agent.
E. Domain Controller Agent.

QUESTION 48

A FortiGate unit can create a secure connection to a client using SSL VPN in tunnel mode.
Which of the following statements are correct regarding the use of tunnel mode SSL VPN? (Select all that apply.)

A. Split tunneling can be enabled when using tunnel mode SSL VPN.
B. Software must be downloaded to the web client to be able to use a tunnel mode SSL VPN.
C. Users attempting to create a tunnel mode SSL VPN connection must be members of a configured user group on the FortiGate unit.
D. Tunnel mode SSL VPN requires the FortiClient software to be installed on the user's computer.
E. The source IP address used by the client for the tunnel mode SSL VPN is assigned by the FortiGate unit.

QUESTION 49

An end user logs into the SSL VPN portal and selects the Tunnel Mode option by clicking on the "Connect" button. The administrator has not enabled split tunneling and so the end user must access the Internet through the SSL VPN Tunnel. Which firewall policies are needed to allow the end user to not only access the internal network but also reach the Internet?

A.

	Status	ID	Source	Destination	Schedule	Service	Action
ssl.root -> internal (1)							
	✔	2	all	all	always	ANY	ACCEPT
ssl.root -> wan1 (1)							
	✔	3	all	all	always	ANY	ACCEPT
wan1 -> internal (1)							
	✔	1	all	all	always	ANY	SSL-VPN
Implicit (1)							

B.

	Status	ID	Source	Destination	Schedule	Service	Action
ssl.root -> internal (1)							
	✔	2	all	all	always	ANY	SSL-VPN
ssl.root -> wan1 (1)							
	✔	3	all	all	always	ANY	SSL-VPN
wan1 -> internal (1)							
	✔	1	all	all	always	ANY	SSL-VPN
Implicit (1)							

C.

	Status	ID	Source	Destination	Schedule	Service	Action
wan1 -> internal (1)							
	✔	1	all	all	always	ANY	SSL-VPN
wan1 -> wan1 (1)							
	✔	2	all	all	always	ANY	SSL-VPN
Implicit (1)							

D.

	Status	ID	Source	Destination	Schedule	Service	Action
wan1 -> internal (1)							
	✔	1	all	all	always	ANY	ACCEPT
wan1 -> wan1 (1)							
	✔	2	all	all	always	ANY	ACCEPT
Implicit (1)							

QUESTION 50

Which of the following antivirus and attack definition update features are supported by FortiGate units? (Select all that apply.)

A. Manual, user-initiated updates from the FortiGuard Distribution Network.
B. Hourly, daily, or weekly scheduled antivirus and attack definition and antivirus engine updates from the FortiGuard Distribution Network.
C. Push updates from the FortiGuard Distribution Network.
D. Update status including version numbers, expiry dates, and most recent update dates and times.

QUESTION 51

By default the Intrusion Protection System (IPS) on a FortiGate unit is set to perform which action?

A. Block all network attacks.
B. Block the most common network attacks.
C. Allow all traffic.
D. Allow and log all traffic.

QUESTION 52

A FortiGate unit can scan for viruses on which types of network traffic? (Select all that apply.)

A. POP3
B. FTP
C. SMTP
D. SNMP
E. NetBios

QUESTION 53

Which of the following statements regarding Banned Words are correct? (Select all that apply.)

A. The FortiGate unit can scan web pages and email messages for instances of banned words.
B. When creating a banned word list, an administrator can indicate either specific words or patterns.
C. Banned words can be expressed as wildcards or regular expressions.
D. Content is automatically blocked if a single instance of a banned word appears.
E. The FortiGate unit includes a pre-defined library of common banned words.

QUESTION 54

Which statement is correct regarding virus scanning on a FortiGate unit?

A. Virus scanning is enabled by default.
B. Fortinet Customer Support enables virus scanning remotely for you.
C. Virus scanning must be enabled in a protection profile and the protection profile must be assigned to a firewall policy.
D. Enabling virus scanning in a protection profile enables virus scanning for all traffic flowing through the FortiGate.

QUESTION 55

Which of the following statements is correct regarding URL Filtering on the FortiGate unit?

A. The available actions for URL Filtering are Allow and Block.
B. Multiple URL Filter lists can be added to a single Web filter profile.
C. A FortiGuard Web Filtering Override match will override a block action in the URL filter list.
D. The available actions for URL Filtering are Allow, Block and Exempt.

QUESTION 56

Which of the following statements is correct regarding URL Filtering on the FortiGate unit?

A. The FortiGate unit can filter URLs based on patterns using text and regular expressions.
B. The available actions for URL Filtering are Allow and Block.
C. Multiple URL Filter lists can be added to a single Web filter profile.
D. A FortiGuard Web Filtering Override match will override a block action in the URL filter list.

QUESTION 57

Which of the following Regular Expression patterns will make the term "bad language" case insensitive?

A. [bad language]
B. /bad language/i
C. i/bad language/
D. "bad language"
E. /bad language/c

QUESTION 58

SSL content inspection is enabled on the FortiGate unit. Which of the following steps is required to prevent a user from being presented with a web browser warning when accessing an SSL-encrypted website?

A. The root certificate of the FortiGate SSL proxy must be imported into the local certificate store on the user's workstation.
B. Disable the strict server certificate check in the web browser under Internet Options.
C. Enable transparent proxy mode on the FortiGate unit.
D. Enable NTLM authentication on the FortiGate unit. NTLM authentication suppresses the certificate warning messages in the web browser.

QUESTION 59

Which of the following statements describes the method of creating a policy to block access to an FTP site?

A. Enable Web Filter URL blocking and add the URL of the FTP site to the URL Block list.
B. Create a firewall policy with destination address set to the IP address of the FTP site, the Service set to FTP, and the Action set to Deny.
C. Create a firewall policy with a protection profile containing the Block FTP option enabled.
D. None of the above.

QUESTION 60

UTM features can be applied to which of the following items?

A. Firewall policies
B. User groups
C. Policy routes
D. Address groups

QUESTION 61

Each UTM feature has configurable UTM objects such as sensors, profiles or lists that define how the feature will function. How are UTM features applied to traffic?

A. One or more UTM features are enabled in a firewall policy.
B. In the system configuration for that UTM feature, you can identify the policies to which the feature is to be applied.
C. Enable the appropriate UTM objects and identify one of them as the default.
D. For each UTM object, identify which policy will use it.

QUESTION 62

If no firewall policy is specified between two FortiGate interfaces and zones are not used, which of the following statements describes the action taken on traffic flowing between these interfaces?

A. The traffic is blocked.
B. The traffic is passed.
C. The traffic is passed and logged.
D. The traffic is blocked and logged.

QUESTION 63

In which order are firewall policies processed on the FortiGate unit?

A. They are processed from the top down as they appear in Web Config.
B. They are processed based on the policy ID number shown in the left hand column of the policy window.
C. They are processed using a policy hierarchy scheme that allows for multiple decision branching.
D. They are processed based on a priority value assigned through the priority column in the policy window.

QUESTION 64

File blocking rules are applied before which of the following?

A. Firewall policy processing
B. Virus scanning
C. Web URL filtering
D. White/Black list filtering

QUESTION 65

Which of the following pieces of information can be included in the Destination Address field of a firewall policy?

A. An IP address pool, a virtual IP address, an actual IP address, and an IP address group.

B. A virtual IP address, an actual IP address, and an IP address group.

C. An actual IP address and an IP address group.

D. Only an actual IP address.

QUESTION 66

FortiGate units are preconfigured with four default protection profiles. These protection profiles are used to control the type of content inspection to be performed. What action must be taken for one of these profiles to become active?

A. The protection profile must be assigned to a firewall policy.
B. The "Use Protection Profile" option must be selected in the Web Config tool under the sections for AntiVirus, IPS, WebFilter, and AntiSpam.
C. The protection profile must be set as the Active Protection Profile.
D. All of the above.

QUESTION 67

A FortiGate 60 unit is configured for your small office. The DMZ interface is connected to a network containing a web server and email server. The Internal interface is connected to a network containing 10 user workstations and the WAN1 interface is connected to your ISP.
You want to configure firewall policies so that your users can send and receive email messages to the email server on the DMZ network. You also want the email server to be able to retrieve email messages from an email server hosted by your ISP using the POP3 protocol.
Which policies must be created for this communication? (Select all that apply.)

A. Internal > DMZ
B. DMZ > Internal
C. Internal > WAN1
D. WAN1 > Internal
E. DMZ > WAN1
F. WAN1 > DMZ

QUESTION 68

The ordering of firewall policies is very important. Policies can be re-ordered within the FortiGate Web Config and also using the CLI. The command used in the CLI to perform this function is_____.

A. set order
B. edit policy
C. reorder
D. move

QUESTION 69
Which of the following statements best describes the green status indicators that appear next to different FortiGuard Distribution Network services as illustrated in the exhibit?

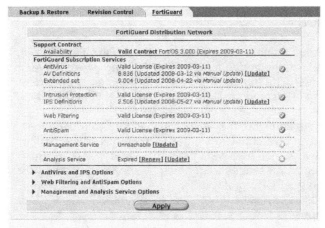

A. They indicate that the FortiGate unit is able to connect to the FortiGuard Distribution Network.
B. They indicate that the FortiGate unit has the latest updates that are available from the FortiGuard Distribution Network.
C. They indicate that updates are available and should be downloaded from the FortiGuard Distribution Network to the FortiGate unit.
D. They indicate that the FortiGate unit is in the process of downloading updates from the FortiGuard Distribution Network.

QUESTION 70

A FortiGate 100 unit is configured to receive push updates from the FortiGuard Distribution Network, however, updates are not being received. Which of the following statements are possible reasons for this? (Select all that apply.)

A. The external facing interface of the FortiGate unit is configured to use DHCP.
B. The FortiGate unit has not been registered.
C. There is a NAT device between the FortiGate unit and the FortiGuard Distribution Network.
D. The FortiGate unit is in Transparent mode.

QUESTION 71

Caching improves performance by reducing FortiGate unit requests to the FortiGuard server.
Which of the following statements are correct regarding the caching of FortiGuard responses? (Select all that apply.)

A. Caching is available for web filtering, antispam, and IPS requests.
B. The cache uses a small portion of the FortiGate system memory.
C. When the cache is full, the least recently used IP address or URL is deleted from the cache.
D. An administrator can configure the number of seconds to store information in the cache before the FortiGate unit contacts the FortiGuard server again.
E. The size of the cache will increase to accomodate any number of cached queries.

QUESTION 72

Which of the following products can be installed on a computer running Windows XP to provide personal firewall protection, antivirus protection, web and mail filtering, spam filtering, and VPN functionality?

A. FortiGate
B. FortiAnalyzer
C. FortiClient
D. FortiManager
E. FortiReporter

QUESTION 73

A FortiAnalyzer device could use which security method to secure the transfer of log data from FortiGate devices?

A. SSL
B. IPSec
C. direct serial connection
D. S/MIME

QUESTION 74

Which of the following Fortinet products can receive updates from the FortiGuard Distribution Network? (Select all that apply.)

A. FortiGate
B. FortiClient
C. FortiMail
D. FortiAnalyzer

QUESTION 75

Which Fortinet products & features could be considered part of a comprehensive solution to monitor and prevent the leakage of senstive data? (Select all that apply.)

A. Archive non-compliant outgoing e-mails using FortiMail.
B. Restrict unofficial methods of transferring files such as P2P using Application Control lists on a FortiGate.
C. Monitor database activity using FortiAnalyzer.
D. Apply a DLP sensor to a firewall policy.
E. Configure FortiClient to prevent files flagged as sensitive from being copied to a USB disk.

QUESTION 76

Which of the following statements are correct regarding logging to memory on a FortiGate unit? (Select all that apply.)

A. When the system has reached its capacity for log messages, the FortiGate unit will stop logging to memory.
B. When the system has reached its capacity for log messages, the FortiGate unit overwrites the oldest messages.
C. If the FortiGate unit is reset or loses power, log entries captured to memory will be lost.
D. None of the above.

QUESTION 77

An administrator configures a FortiGate unit in Transparent mode on the 192.168.11.0 subnet. Automatic Discovery is enabled to detect any available FortiAnalyzers on the network. Which of the following FortiAnalyzers will be detected? (Select all that apply.)

A. 192.168.11.100
B. 192.168.11.251
C. 192.168.10.100
D. 192.168.10.251

QUESTION 78

Which of the following items does NOT support the Logging feature?

A. File Filter
B. Application control
C. Session timeouts
D. Administrator activities
E. Web URL filtering

QUESTION 79

DLP archiving gives the ability to store session transaction data on a FortiAnalyzer unit for which of the following types of network traffic? (Select all that apply.)

A. SNMP
B. IPSec
C. SMTP
D. POP3
E. HTTP

QUESTION 80

Alert emails enable the FortiGate unit to send email notifications to an email address upon detection of a pre-defined event type. Which of the following are some of the available event types in Web Config? (Select all that apply.)

A. Intrusion detected.
B. Successful firewall authentication.
C. Oversized file detected.
D. DHCP address assigned.
E. FortiGuard Web Filtering rating error detected.

QUESTION 81

FSSO provides a single sign on solution to authenticate users transparently to a FortiGate unit using credentials stored in Windows Active Directory.
Which of the following statements are correct regarding FSSO in a Windows domain environment when NTLM and Polling Mode are not used? (Select all that apply.)

A. An FSSO Collector Agent must be installed on every domain controller.
B. An FSSO Domain Controller Agent must be installed on every domain controller.
C. The FSSO Domain Controller Agent will regularly update user logon information on the FortiGate unit.
D. The FSSO Collector Agent will retrieve user information from the Domain Controller Agent and will send the user logon information to the FortiGate unit.
E. For non-domain computers, the only way to allow FSSO authentication is to install an FSSO client.

QUESTION 82

Which of the following represents the correct order of criteria
used for the selection of a Master unit within a FortiGate High
Availability (HA) cluster when master override is disabled?

A. 1. port monitor, 2. unit priority, 3. up time, 4. serial number
B. 1. port monitor, 2. up time, 3. unit priority, 4. serial number
C. 1. unit priority, 2. up time, 3. port monitor, 4. serial number
D. 1. up time, 2. unit priority, 3. port monitor, 4. serial number

QUESTION 83

In a High Availability cluster operating in Active-Active mode,
which of the following correctly describes the path taken by the
SYN packet of an HTTP session that is offloaded to a
subordinate unit?

A. Request: Internal Host; Master FortiGate; Slave FortiGate;
   Internet; Web Server
B. Request: Internal Host; Master FortiGate; Slave FortiGate;
   Master FortiGate; Internet; Web Server
C. Request: Internal Host; Slave FortiGate; Internet; Web
   Server
D. Request: Internal Host; Slave FortiGate; Master FortiGate;
   Internet; Web Server

QUESTION 84

Which of the following statements are correct regarding virtual domains (VDOMs)? (Select all that apply.)

A. VDOMs divide a single FortiGate unit into two or more virtual units that function as multiple, independent units.
B. A management VDOM handles SNMP, logging, alert email, and FDN-based updates.
C. VDOMs share firmware versions, as well as antivirus and IPS databases.
D. Only administrative users with a 'super_admin' profile will be able to enter multiple VDOMs to make configuration changes.

QUESTION 85

What advantages are there in using a hub-and-spoke IPSec VPN configuration instead of a fully-meshed set of IPSec tunnels? (Select all that apply.)

A. Using a hub and spoke topology is required to achieve full redundancy.
B. Using a hub and spoke topology simplifies configuration because fewer tunnels are required.
C. Using a hub and spoke topology provides stronger encryption.
D. The routing at a spoke is simpler, compared to a meshed node.

QUESTION 86

Data Leak Prevention archiving gives the ability to store files and message data onto a FortiAnalyzer unit for which of the following types of network traffic? (Select all that apply.)

A. SNMP
B. IPSec
C. SMTP
D. POP3
E. HTTP

QUESTION 87

Which of the following statements are correct regarding Application Control?

A. Application Control is based on the IPS engine.
B. Application Control is based on the AV engine.
C. Application Control can be applied to SSL encrypted traffic.
D. Application Control cannot be applied to SSL encrypted traffic.

QUESTION 88

Examine the exhibit shown below then answer the question that follows it.

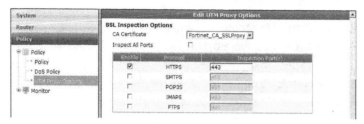

Within the UTM Proxy Options, the CA certificate Fortinet_CA_SSLProxy defines which of the following:

A. FortiGate unit's encryption certificate used by the SSL proxy.
B. FortiGate unit's signing certificate used by the SSL proxy.
C. FortiGuard's signing certificate used by the SSL proxy.
D. FortiGuard's encryption certificate used by the SSL proxy.

QUESTION 89

For Data Leak Prevention, which of the following describes the difference between the block and quarantine actions?

A. A block action prevents the transaction. A quarantine action blocks all future transactions, regardless of the protocol.
B. A block action prevents the transaction. A quarantine action archives the data.
C. A block action has a finite duration. A quarantine action must be removed by an administrator.
D. A block action is used for known users. A quarantine action is used for unknown users.

QUESTION 90

How can DLP file filters be configured to detect Office 2010 files? (Select all that apply.)

A. File TypE. Microsoft Office(msoffice)
B. File TypE. Archive(zip)
C. File TypE. Unknown Filetype(unknown)
D. File NamE. "*.ppt", "*.doc", "*.xls"
E. File NamE. "*.pptx", "*.docx", "*.xlsx"

QUESTION 91

Examine the Exhibits shown below, then answer the question that follows. Review the following DLP Sensor (Exhibit 1):

Seq #	Type	Action	Services	Arc
1	File Type	Log Only	SMTP, POP3, IMAP, HTTP, NNTP	Dis.
2	File Type	Quarantine Interface	SMTP, POP3, IMAP, HTTP, NNTP	Dis.
3	File Type	Block	SMTP, POP3, IMAP, HTTP, NNTP	Dis.

Review the following File Filter list for rule #1 (Exhibit 2):

Filter Type	Filter
File Type	Audio (mp3)
File Type	Audio (wma)
File Type	Audio (wav)

Review the following File Filter list for rule #2 (Exhibit 3):

Filter Type	Filter
File Name Pattern	*.exe

Review the following File Filter list for rule #3 (Exhibit 4):

Filter Type	Filter
File Type	Archive (arj)
File Type	Archive (bzip)
File Type	Archive (cab)
File Type	Archive (zip)

An MP3 file is renamed to 'workbook.exe' and put into a ZIP archive. It is then sent through the FortiGate device over HTTP. It is intercepted and processed by the configuration shown in the above Exhibits 1-4.
Assuming the file is not too large for the File scanning threshold, what action will the FortiGate unit take?

A. The file will be detected by rule #1 as an 'Audio (mp3)', a log entry will be created and it will be allowed to pass through.
B. The file will be detected by rule #2 as a "*.exe", a log entry will be created and the interface that received the traffic will be brought down.
C. The file will be detected by rule #3 as an Archive(zip), blocked, and a log entry will be created.
D. Nothing, the file will go undetected.

QUESTION 92

The eicar test virus is put into a zip archive, which is given the password of "Fortinet" in order to open the archive. Review the configuration in the exhibits shown below; then answer the question that follows.

Exhibit A – Antivirus Profile:

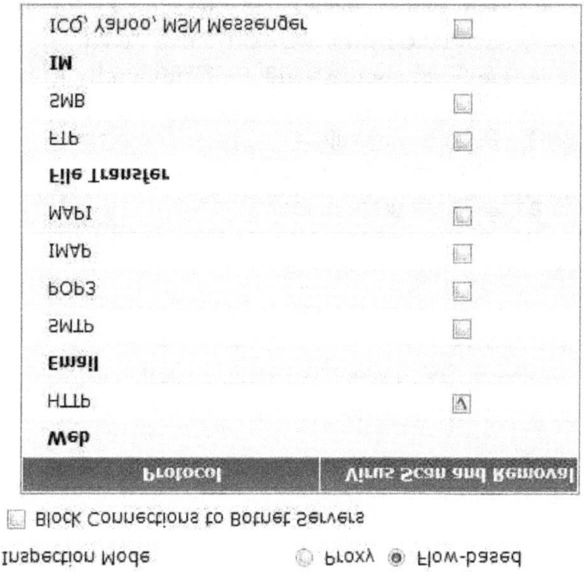

Protocol	Virus Scan and Removal
Web	
HTTP	∨
Email	
SMTP	☐
POP3	☐
IMAP	☐
MAPI	☐
File Transfer	
FTP	☐
SMB	☐
IM	
ICQ, Yahoo, MSN Messenger	☐

☐ Block Connections to Botnet Servers

Inspection Mode   ○ Proxy   ● Flow-based

Exhibit B – Non-default UTM Proxy Options Profile:

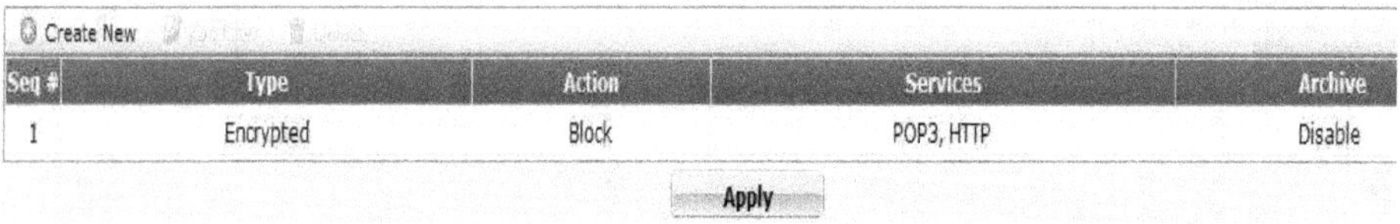

Seq #	Type	Action	Services	Archive
1	Encrypted	Block	POP3, HTTP	Disable

⊕ Create New

Apply

Exhibit C – DLP Profile:

Protocol Port Mapping

Enable	Protocol	Inspection Port(s)
☑	HTTP	○ Any ◉ Specify 8080
☑	SMTP	○ Any ◉ Specify 25
☑	POP3	○ Any ◉ Specify 110
☑	IMAP	○ Any ◉ Specify 143
☑	FTP	○ Any ◉ Specify 21
☑	NNTP	○ Any ◉ Specify 119
☑	MAPI	135
☑	DNS	53

Which of one the following profiles could be enabled in order to prevent the file from passing through the FortiGate device over HTTP on the standard port for that protocol?

A. Only Exhibit A
B. Only Exhibit B
C. Only Exhibit C with default UTM Proxy settings.
D. All of the Exhibits (A, B and C)
E. Only Exhibit C with non-default UTM Proxy settings (Exhibit B).

QUESTION 93

With FSSO, a domain user could authenticate either against the domain controller running the Collector Agent and Domain Controller Agent, or a domain controller running only the Domain Controller Agent.
If you attempt to authenticate with the Secondary Domain Controller running only the Domain Controller Agent, which of the following statements are correct? (Select all that apply.)

A. The login event is sent to the Collector Agent.
B. The FortiGate unit receives the user information from the Domain Controller Agent of the Secondary Controller.
C. The Collector Agent performs the DNS lookup for the authenticated client's IP address.
D. The user cannot be authenticated with the FortiGate device in this manner because each Domain Controller Agent requires a dedicated Collector Agent.

QUESTION 94

What are the requirements for a cluster to maintain TCP connections after device or link failover? (Select all that apply.)

A. Enable session pick-up.
B. Only applies to connections handled by a proxy.
C. Only applies to UDP and ICMP connections.
D. Connections must not be handled by a proxy.

QUESTION 95

Two devices are in an HA cluster, the device hostnames are STUDENT and REMOTE. Exhibit A shows the command output of 'diag sys session stat' for the STUDENT device. Exhibit B shows the command output of 'diag sys session stat' for the REMOTE device.

Exhibit A:

```
STUDENT # diagnose sys session stat
misc info:        session_count=166 setup_rate=68 exp_count=0 clash=0
        memory_tension_drop=0 ephemeral=0/57344 removeable=0  ha_scan=0
delete=0, flush=0, dev_down=0/0
TCP sessions:
        8 in ESTABLISHED state
        3 in SYN_SENT state
        1 in FIN_WAIT state
        139 in TIME_WAIT state
firewall error stat:
error1=00000000
error2=00000000
error3=00000000
error4=00000000
tt=00000000
cont=00000000
ids_recv=00000000
url_recv=00000000
av_recv=00000000
fqdn_count=00000000
tcp reset stat:
        syncqf=0 acceptqf=0 no-listener=2 data=0 ses=0 ips=0
global: ses_limit=0 ses6_limit=0 rt_limit=0 rt6_limit=0

STUDENT #
```

Exhibit B:

```
global: ses_limit=0 ses6_limit=0 rt_limit=0 rt6_limit=0

REMOTE # diagnose sys session stat
misc info:        session_count=11 setup_rate=0 exp_count=0 clash=4
        memory_tension_drop=0 ephemeral=0/57344 removeable=0  ha_scan=0
delete=0, flush=0, dev_down=0/0
TCP sessions:
        2 in ESTABLISHED state
        1 in SYN_SENT state
firewall error stat:
error1=00000000
error2=00000000
error3=00000000
error4=00000000
tt=00000000
cont=00000000
ids_recv=00000000
url_recv=00000000
av_recv=00000000
fqdn_count=00000000
tcp reset stat:
        syncqf=0 acceptqf=0 no-listener=7 data=0 ses=0 ips=0
global: ses_limit=0 ses6_limit=0 rt_limit=0 rt6_limit=0

REMOTE #
```

Given the information provided in the exhibits, which of the
following statements are correct? (Select all that apply.)

A. STUDENT is likely to be the master device.
B. Session-pickup is likely to be enabled.
C. The cluster mode is definitely Active-Passive.
D. There is not enough information to determine the cluster mode.

QUESTION 96

Which of the following statements are correct about the HA diag command diagnose sys ha reset-uptime? (Select all that apply.)

A. The device this command is executed on is likely to switch from master to slave status if master override is disabled.
B. The device this command is executed on is likely to switch from master to slave status if master override is enabled.
C. This command has no impact on the HA algorithm.
D. This command resets the uptime variable used in the HA algorithm so it may cause a new master to become elected.

QUESTION 97

In HA, the option Reserve Management Port for Cluster Member is selected as shown in the Exhibit below.

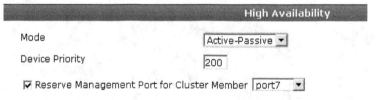

Which of the following statements are correct regarding this setting? (Select all that apply.)

A. Interface settings on port7 will not be synchronized with other cluster members.
B. The IP address assigned to this interface must not overlap with the IP address subnet assigned to another interface.
C. Port7 appears in the routing table.

D. A gateway address may be configured for port7.

E. When connecting to port7 you always connect to the master device.

QUESTION 98

In HA, what is the effect of the Disconnect Cluster Member

Disconnect Cluster Member
Serial Number FGVM010000006268
Interface port3 ▾
IP/Netmask 10.0.1.251/24
OK Cancel

command as given in the Exhibit.

A. The HA mode changes to standalone.

B. Port3 is configured with an IP address for management access.

C. The Firewall rules are purged on the disconnected unit.

D. All other interface IP settings are maintained.

QUESTION 99

Two FortiGate devices fail to form an HA cluster, the device hostnames are STUDENT and REMOTE. Exhibit A shows the command output of 'show system ha' for the STUDENT device. Exhibit B shows the command output of 'show system ha' for the REMOTE device.

Exhibit A:

```
Max number of virtual domains: 10
Virtual domains status: 1 in NAT mode, 0 in TP mode
Virtual domain configuration: disable
FIPS-CC mode: disable
Current HA mode: a-p, master
Branch point: 128
Release Version Information: GA
System time: Thu Jan 24 08:34:19 2013

STUDENT #
STUDENT #
STUDENT #
STUDENT #
STUDENT #
STUDENT # show system ha
config system ha
    set mode a-p
    set password ENC 9FHCYwOJXK9z8wGQkUnUsREWBruVcMJ5NUVE3oV5otyn+4dsgx4CnV1GRJ8
McEECpiT32/3dCmIuYIDgW2sE+1AlkHfADOV/r5DkaqGnbj15XV/a
    set hbdev "port2" 50
    set override disable
    set priority 200
end

STUDENT # _
```

Exhibit B

```
global: ses_limit=0 ses6_limit=0 rt_limit=0 rt6_limit=0

REMOTE # diagnose sys session stat
misc info:        session_count=11 setup_rate=0 exp_count=0 clash=4
       memory_tension_drop=0 ephemeral=0/57344 removeable=0  ha_scan=0
delete=0, flush=0, dev_down=0/0
TCP sessions:
        2 in ESTABLISHED state
        1 in SYN_SENT state
firewall error stat:
error1=00000000
error2=00000000
error3=00000000
error4=00000000
tt=00000000
cont=00000000
ids_recv=00000000
url_recv=00000000
av_recv=00000000
fqdn_count=00000000
tcp reset stat:
        syncqf=0 acceptqf=0 no-listener=7 data=0 ses=0 ips=0
global: ses_limit=0 ses6_limit=0 rt_limit=0 rt6_limit=0

REMOTE # _
```

Which one of the following is the most likely reason that the cluster fails to form?

A. Password
B. HA mode

C. Hearbeat

D. Override

QUESTION 100

Examine the following log message for IPS and identify the valid responses below. (Select all that apply.)
2012-07-01 09:54:28 oid=2 log_id=18433 type=ips subtype=anomaly pri=alert vd=root severity="critical" src="192.168.3.168" dst="192.168.3.170" src_int="port2" serial=0 status="detected" proto=1 service="icmp" count=1 attack_name="icmp_flood" icmp_id="0xa8a4" icmp_type="0x08" icmp_code="0x00" attack_id=16777316 sensor="1" ref="http://www.fortinet.com/ids/VID16777316" msg="anomaly: icmp_flood, 51 > threshold 50"

A. The target is 192.168.3.168.

B. The target is 192.168.3.170.

C. The attack was detected and blocked.

D. The attack was detected only.

E. The attack was TCP based.

QUESTION 101

Identify the statement which correctly describes the output of the following command:
Diagnose ips anomaly list

A. Lists the configured DoS policy.

B. List the real-time counters for the configured DoS policy.

C. Lists the errors captured when compiling the DoS policy.

QUESTION 102

Review the CLI configuration below for an IPS sensor and
identify the correct statements regarding this configuration from
the choices below. (Select all that apply.) config ips sensor
  edit "LINUX_SERVER"
    set comment "
    set replacemsg-group "

    set log enable config entries edit 1
      set action default set application all set location server
      set log enable
      set log-packet enable set os Linux
      set protocol all
      set quarantine none set severity all
      set status default next
    end next end

A. The sensor will log all server attacks for all operating systems.
B. The sensor will include a PCAP file with a trace of the matching packets in the log message of any matched signature.
C. The sensor will match all traffic from the address object 'LINUX_SERVER'.
D. The sensor will reset all connections that match these signatures.
E. The sensor only filters which IPS signatures to apply to the selected firewall policy

QUESTION 103

Identify the correct properties of a partial mesh VPN
deployment:

A. VPN tunnels interconnect between every single location.
B. VPN tunnels are not configured between every single location.
C. Some locations are reached via a hub location.
D. There are no hub locations in a partial mesh.

QUESTION 104
Review the IPsec phase1 configuration in the Exhibit shown below; then answer the question following it.

Which of the following statements are correct regarding this configuration? (Select all that apply).

A. The phase1 is for a route-based VPN configuration.
B. The phase1 is for a policy-based VPN configuration.
C. The local gateway IP is the address assigned to port1.
D. The local gateway IP address is 10.200.3.1.

QUESTION 105
Review the IPsec Phase2 configuration shown in the Exhibit; then answer the question following it.

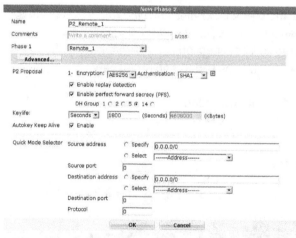

Which of the following statements are correct regarding this configuration? (Select all that apply).

A. The Phase 2 will re-key even if there is no traffic.

B. There will be a DH exchange for each re-key.

C. The sequence number of ESP packets received from the peer will not be checked.

D. Quick mode selectors will default to those used in the firewall policy.

QUESTION 106

Review the static route configuration for IPsec shown in the Exhibit below; then answer the question following it.

Which of the following statements are correct regarding this configuration? (Select all that apply).

A. Remote_1 is a Phase 1 object with interface mode enabled
B. The gateway address is not required because the interface is a point-to-point connection
C. The gateway address is not required because the default route is used
D. Remote_1 is a firewall zone

QUESTION 107

Review the IKE debug output for IPsec shown in the Exhibit below.

```
STUDENT # ike 0: comes 10.200.3.1:500->10.200.1.1:500,ifindex=2....
ike 0: IKEv1 exchange=Informational id=9e2606ac7ae83d7a/612da78d3ab3f945:15b10705 len=92
ike 0: in 9E2606AC7AE83D7A612DA78D3AB3F9450810050115B107050000005C26E2A7EC8461AC15E9BBC705B6C1F667A41957AED11FB7003C07A1E11761
37BD934DD38E1A2074348E08FD6B39146C618525C6EC51E2F26885B6BB8E035F52B4
ike 0:Remote_1:10: dec 9E2606AC7AE83D7A612DA78D3AB3F9450810050115B107050000005C0B000018E281874EECF170EB5222D6A4E3A027C71419740
00000002000000001011080289E2606AC7AE83D7A612DA78D3AB3F9450000009C17511ED8EE549507
ike 0:Remote_1:10: notify msg received: R-U-THERE
ike 0:Remote_1:10: enc 9E2606AC7AE83D7A612DA78D3AB3F94508100501734C5CDF000000540B0000181C047F014CBEF1B0EC8DA915F3818AEBC0D995E
A0000002000000001011080299E2606AC7AE83D7A612DA78D3AB3F9450000009C
ike 0:Remote_1:10: out 9E2606AC7AE83D7A612DA78D3AB3F94508100501734C5CDF0000005CB3CC431065A1737144D02F1AACE79C1BE712B042558ACC3
BB84E5FA7A967FE99C7E731057FF33728BB42AA983E79C919DA9B64EBCE087EF0A02666C1FBD2C62F
ike 0:Remote_1:10: sent IKE msg (R-U-THERE-ACK): 10.200.1.1:500->10.200.3.1:500, len=92, id=9e2606ac7ae83d7a/612da78d3ab3f945:
734c5cdf
ike 0:Remote_1: link is idle 2 10.200.1.1->10.200.3.1:500 dpd=1 seqno=34
```

Which one of the following statements is correct regarding this output?

A. The output is a Phase 1 negotiation.

B. The output is a Phase 2 negotiation.

C. The output captures the Dead Peer Detection messages.

D. The output captures the Dead Gateway Detection packets.

QUESTION 108

Review the IPsec diagnostics output of the command diag vpn tunnel list shown in the Exhibit.

```
STUDENT # diagnose vpn tunnel list
list all ipsec tunnel in vd 0
------------------------------------------------------
name=Remote_1 ver=1 serial=1 10.200.1.1:0->10.200.3.1:0 lgwy=static tun=intf mode=auto bound_if=2
proxyid_num=1 child_num=0 refcnt=6 ilast=2 olast=2
stat: rxp=8 txp=8 rxb=960 txb=480
dpd: mode=active on=1 idle=5000ms retry=3 count=0 seqno=128
natt: mode=none draft=0 interval=0 remote_port=0
proxyid=P2_Remote_1 proto=0 sa=1 ref=2 auto_negotiate=0 serial=1
  src: 0:0.0.0.0/0.0.0.0:0
  dst: 0:0.0.0.0/0.0.0.0:0
  SA: ref=3 options=0000000f type=00 soft=0 mtu=1412 expire=1486 replaywin=1024 seqno=1
  life: type=01 bytes=0/0 timeout=1753/1800
  dec: spi=b95a77fe esp=aes key=32 84ed410c1bb9f61e535a49563c4e7646e9e110628b79b0ac034e2d05e3b6a0e6
       ah=sha1 key=20 6bddbfad7161237daa46c19725dd0292b062dda5
  enc: spi=9293e7d4 esp=aes key=32 951befd87860cdb55b98b170a17dcb75f77bd541bdc3a1847e54c78c0d43aa13
       ah=sha1 key=20 8a5bedd6a0ce0f8daf7591601acfe2c618a0d4e2
------------------------------------------------------
name=Remote_2 ver=1 serial=2 10.200.2.1:0->10.200.4.1:0 lgwy=static tun=intf mode=auto bound_if=3
proxyid_num=1 child_num=0 refcnt=6 ilast=0 olast=0
stat: rxp=0 txp=0 rxb=0 txb=0
dpd: mode=active on=1 idle=5000ms retry=3 count=0 seqno=0
natt: mode=none draft=0 interval=0 remote_port=0
proxyid=P2_Remote_2 proto=0 sa=1 ref=2 auto_negotiate=0 serial=1
  src: 0:0.0.0.0/0.0.0.0:0
  dst: 0:0.0.0.0/0.0.0.0:0
  SA: ref=3 options=0000000f type=00 soft=0 mtu=1280 expire=1732 replaywin=1024 seqno=1
  life: type=01 bytes=0/0 timeout=1749/1800
  dec: spi=b95a77ff esp=aes key=32 582af59d71635b835c9208878e0e3f3fe31baldfd88ff83ca9babled66ac325e
       ah=sha1 key=20 0d951e62a1bcb63232df6d0fb86df49ab714f53b
  enc: spi=9293e7d5 esp=aes key=32 eeeecacf3a58161f3390fa612b794c778654c86aef51fbc7542906223d56ebb3
       ah=sha1 key=20 09eaa3085bc30a59091f182eb5d11550385b6304
```

Which of the following statements is correct regarding this output? (Select one answer).

A. One tunnel is rekeying

B. Two tunnels are rekeying

C. Two tunnels are up

D. One tunnel is up

QUESTION 109

Review the configuration for FortiClient IPsec shown in the Exhibit below.

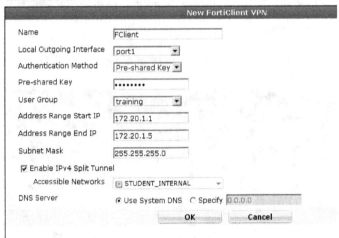

Which of the following statements is correct regarding this configuration?

A. The connecting VPN client will install a route to a destination corresponding to the STUDENT_INTERNAL address object

B. The connecting VPN client will install a default route

C. The connecting VPN client will install a route to the 172.20.1.[1-5] address range

D. The connecting VPN client will connect in web portal mode and no route will be installed

QUESTION 110

Review the IPsec diagnostics output of the command diag vpn tunnel list shown in the Exhibit below.

```
STUDENT # diagnose vpn tunnel list
list all ipsec tunnel in vd 0
------------------------------------------------------------
name=FClient_0 ver=1 serial=3 10.200.1.1:4500->10.200.3.1:64916 lguy=static tun=intf mode=dial_inst bound_if=2
parent=FClient index=0
proxyid_num=1 child_num=0 refcnt=8 ilast=2 olast=2
stat: rxp=59 txp=0 rxb=15192 txb=0
dpd: mode=active on=1 idle=5000ms retry=3 count=0 seqno=10
natt: mode=keepalive draft=32 interval=10 remote_port=64916
proxyid=FClient proto=0 sa=1 ref=2 auto_negotiate=0 serial=1
  src: 0:0.0.0.0-255.255.255.255:0
  dst: 0:172.20.1.1-172.20.1.1:0
  SA: ref=3 options=00000006 type=00 soft=0 mtu=1280 expire=1717 replaywin=1024 seqno=1
  life: type=01 bytes=0/0 timeout=1791/1800
  dec: spi=a29046e9 esp=3des key=24 0525830c6fd67ca37e9d6dad174d175e24f97c3b87f428fa
      ah=sha1 key=20 982f8ba194f3f797773efc605c8321b728dabf1d
  enc: spi=19be4052 esp=3des key=24 da597cb7fec913528f8598d1aa7ecd17156a2a7a4afeeb4c
      ah=sha1 key=20 9e2c5d0fc055fa0149bc66024732e9a85bbe8016
------------------------------------------------------------
```

Which of the following statements are correct regarding this output? (Select all that apply.)

A. The connecting client has been allocated address 172.20.1.1.

B. In the Phase 1 settings, dead peer detection is enabled.

C. The tunnel is idle.

D. The connecting client has been allocated address 10.200.3.1.

QUESTION 111

Examine the Exhibit shown below; then answer the question following it.

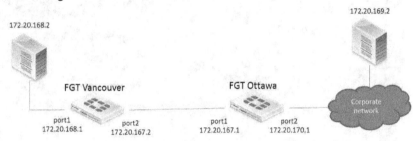

172.20.169.2

172.20.168.2

FGT Vancouver

FGT Ottawa

port1
172.20.168.1

port2
172.20.167.2

port1
172.20.167.1

port2
172.20.170.1

Corporate
network

In this scenario, the Fortigate unit in Ottawa has the following routing table: S* 0.0.0.0/0 [10/0] via 172.20.170.254, port2

C   172.20.167.0/24 is directly connected, port1 C
     172.20.170.0/24 is directly connected, port2
Sniffer tests show that packets sent from the Source IP address 172.20.168.2 to the Destination IP address 172.20.169.2 are being dropped by the FortiGate unit located in Ottaw

A. Which of the following correctly describes the cause for the dropped packets?
B. The forward policy check.
C. The reverse path forwarding check.
D. The subnet 172.20.169.0/24 is NOT in the Ottawa FortiGate unit's routing table.
E. The destination workstation 172.20.169.2 does NOT have the subnet 172.20.168.0/24 in its routing table.

QUESTION 112

Examine the two static routes to the same destination subnet
172.20.168.0/24 as shown below; then answer the question
following it. config router static
edit 1
set dst 172.20.168.0 255.255.255.0
set distance 20
set priority 10 set device port1 next
edit 2
set dst 172.20.168.0 255.255.255.0
set distance 20
set priority 20 set device port2 next
end
Which of the following statements correctly describes the static
routing configuration provided above?

A. The FortiGate unit will evenly share the traffic to
   172.20.168.0/24 through both routes.
B. The FortiGate unit will share the traffic to 172.20.168.0/24
   through both routes, but the port2 route will carry
   approximately twice as much of the traffic.
C. The FortiGate unit will send all the traffic to 172.20.168.0/24
   through port1.
D. Only the route that is using port1 will show up in the routing
   table.

QUESTION 113

Examine the Exhibit shown below; then answer the question following it.

FGT Vancouver

port2
172.21.1.1/16

port1
172.11.11.1/24

Corporate
network

FGT Ottawa

Port1
172.11.12.1/24

port2
172.20.1.1/24

The Vancouver FortiGate unit initially had the following information in its routing table:
S   172.20.0.0/16 [10/0] via 172.21.1.2, port2
C   172.21.0.0/16 is directly connected, port2 C
     172.11.11.0/24 is directly connected, port1
Afterwards, the following static route was added:
config router static edit 6
set dst 172.20.1.0 255.255.255.0
set pririoty 0
set device port1
set gateway 172.11.12.1 next
end
Since this change, the new static route is NOT showing up in the routing table. Given the information provided, which of the following describes the cause of this problem?

A. The subnet 172.20.1.0/24 is overlapped with the subnet of one static route that is already in the routing table (172.20.0.0/16), so, we need to enable allow- subnet-overlap first.

B. The 'gateway' IP address is NOT in the same subnet as the IP address of port1.

C. The priority is 0, which means that the route will remain inactive.

D. The static route configuration is missing the distance setting.

QUESTION 114

Examine the static route configuration shown below; then answer the question following it. config router static
edit 1
set dst 172.20.1.0 255.255.255.0
set device port1
set gateway 172.11.12.1
set distance 10
set weight 5 next
edit 2
set dst 172.20.1.0 255.255.255.0
set blackhole enable set distance 5
set weight 10 next
end
Which of the following statements correctly describes the static routing configuration provided? (Select all that apply.)

A. All traffic to 172.20.1.0/24 will always be dropped by the FortiGate unit.
B. As long as port1 is up, all the traffic to 172.20.1.0/24 will be routed by the static route number 1. If the interface port1 is down, the traffic will be routed using the blackhole route.
C. The FortiGate unit will NOT create a session entry in the session table when the traffic is being routed by the blackhole route.
D. The FortiGate unit will create a session entry in the session table when the traffic is being routed by the blackhole route.
E. Traffic to 172.20.1.0/24 will be shared through both routes.

QUESTION 115

In the case of TCP traffic, which of the following correctly describes the routing table lookups performed by a FortiGate unit when searching for a suitable gateway?

A. A look-up is done only when the first packet coming from the client (SYN) arrives.
B. A look-up is done when the first packet coming from the client (SYN) arrives, and a second is performed when the first packet coming from the server (SYNC/ ACK) arrives.
C. A look-up is done only during the TCP 3-way handshake (SYNC, SYNC/ACK, ACK).
D. A look-up is always done each time a packet arrives, from either the server or the client side.

QUESTION 116

Shown below is a section of output from the debug command diag ip arp list.
index=2 ifname=port1 172.20.187.150 00:09:0f:69:03:7e state=00000004 use=4589 confirm=4589 update=2422 ref=1 In the output provided, which of the following best describes the IP address 172.20.187.150?

A. It is the primary IP address of the port1 interface.
B. It is one of the secondary IP addresses of the port1 interface.
C. It is the IP address of another network device located in the same LAN segment as the FortiGate unit's port1 interface.

QUESTION 117

Review the output of the command get router info routing-table database shown in the Exhibit below; then answer the question following it.

```
STUDENT # get router info routing-table database
Codes: K - kernel, C - connected, S - static, R - RIP, B - BGP
       O - OSPF, IA - OSPF inter area
       N1 - OSPF NSSA external type 1, N2 - OSPF NSSA external type 2
       E1 - OSPF external type 1, E2 - OSPF external type 2
       i - IS-IS, L1 - IS-IS level-1, L2 - IS-IS level-2, ia - IS-IS inter area
       > - selected route, * - FIB route, p - stale info

S     *> 0.0.0.0/0 [10/0] via 10.200.1.254, port1
      *>           [10/0] via 10.200.2.254, port2, [5/0]
C     *> 10.0.1.0/24 is directly connected, port3
S        10.0.2.0/24 [20/0] is directly connected, Remote_2
S     *> 10.0.2.0/24 [10/0] is directly connected, Remote_1
C     *> 10.200.1.0/24 is directly connected, port1
C     *> 10.200.2.0/24 is directly connected, port2
```

Which of the following statements are correct regarding this output? (Select all that apply).

A. There will be six routes in the routing table.
B. There will be seven routes in the routing table.
C. There will be two default routes in the routing table.
D. There will be two routes for the 10.0.2.0/24 subnet in the routing table.

QUESTION 118

Which of the following statements is correct regarding the NAC Quarantine feature?

A. With NAC quarantine, files can be quarantined not only as a result of antivirus scanning, but also for other forms of content inspection such as IPS and DLP.

B. NAC quarantine does a client check on workstations before they are permitted to have administrative access to FortiGate.

C. NAC quarantine allows administrators to isolate clients whose network activity poses a security risk.

D. If you chose the quarantine action, you must decide whether the quarantine type is NAC quarantine or File quarantine.

QUESTION 119

Which of the following DLP actions will override any other action?

A. Exempt
B. Quarantine Interface
C. Block
D. None

QUESTION 120

Which of the following DLP actions will always be performed if it is selected?
A. Archive
B. Quarantine Interface
C. Ban Sender
D. Block
E. None
F. Ban
G. Quarantine IP Address

QUESTION 121

The transfer of encrypted files or the use of encrypted protocols between users and servers on the internet can frustrate the efforts of administrators attempting to monitor traffic passing through the FortiGate unit and ensuring user compliance to corporate rules.
Which of the following items will allow the administrator to control the transfer of encrypted data through the FortiGate unit? (Select all that apply.)

A. Encrypted protocols can be scanned through the use of the SSL proxy.
B. DLP rules can be used to block the transmission of encrypted files.
C. Firewall authentication can be enabled in the firewall policy, preventing the use of encrypted communications channels.
D. Application control can be used to monitor the use of encrypted protocols; alerts can be sent to the administrator through email when the use of encrypted protocols is attempted.

QUESTION 122

A DLP rule with an action of Exempt has been matched against traffic passing through the FortiGate unit. Which of the following statements is correct regarding how this transaction will be handled by the FortiGate unit?

A. Any other matched DLP rules will be ignored with the exception of Archiving.
B. Future files whose characteristics match this file will bypass DLP scanning.
C. The traffic matching the DLP rule will bypass antivirus scanning.
D. The client IP address will be added to a white list.

QUESTION 123

The following diagnostic output is displayed in the CLI: diag firewall auth list

policy iD. 9, srC. 192.168.3.168, action: accept, timeout: 13427

user: forticlient_chk_only, group:
flag (80020): auth timeout_ext, flag2 (40): exact group iD. 0, av group: 0
----- 1 listed, 0 filtered ------
Based on this output, which of the following statements is correct?

A. Firewall policy 9 has endpoint compliance enabled but not firewall authentication.
B. The client check that is part of an SSL VPN connection attempt failed.
C. This user has been associated with a guest profile as evidenced by the group id of 0.
D. An auth-keepalive value has been enabled.

QUESTION 124

Which of the following cannot be used in conjunction with the endpoint compliance check?

A. HTTP Challenge Redirect to a Secure Channel (HTTPS) in the Authentication Settings.
B. Any form of firewall policy authentication.
C. WAN optimization.
D. Traffic shaping.

QUESTION 125

SSL Proxy is used to decrypt the SSL-encrypted traffic. After decryption, where is the traffic buffered in preparation for content inspection?

A. The file is buffered by the application proxy.
B. The file is buffered by the SSL proxy.
C. In the upload direction, the file is buffered by the SSL proxy. In the download direction, the file is buffered by the application proxy.
D. No file buffering is needed since a stream-based scanning approach is used for SSL content inspection.

QUESTION 126

Which of the following statements correctly describes the deepscan option for HTTPS?

A. When deepscan is disabled, only the web server certificate is inspected; no decryption of content occurs.
B. Enabling deepscan will perform further checks on the server certificate.
C. Deepscan is only applicable to mail protocols, where all IP addresses in the header are checked.
D. With deepscan enabled, archived files will be decompressed before scanning for a more comprehensive file inspection.

QUESTION 127

Which of the following tasks fall under the responsibility of the SSL proxy in a typical HTTPS connection? (Select all that apply.)

A. The web client SSL handshake.
B. The web server SSL handshake.
C. File buffering.
D. Communication with the urlfilter process.

QUESTION 128

When the SSL proxy inspects the server certificate for Web Filtering only in SSL Handshake mode, which certificate field is being used to determine the site rating?

A. Common Name
B. Organization
C. Organizational Unit
D. Serial Number
E. Validity

QUESTION 129

When performing a log search on a FortiAnalyzer, it is generally recommended to use the Quick Search option. What is a valid reason for using the Full Search option, instead?

A. The search items you are looking for are not contained in indexed log fields.
B. A quick search only searches data received within the last 24 hours.
C. You want the search to include the FortiAnalyzer's local logs.
D. You want the search to include content archive data as well.

QUESTION 130

Both the FortiGate and FortiAnalyzer units can notify administrators when certain alert conditions are met. Considering this, which of the following statements is NOT correct?

A. On a FortiGate device, the alert condition is based either on the severity level or on the log type, but not on a combination of the two.

B. On a FortiAnalyzer device, the alert condition is based either on the severity level or on the log type, but not on a combination of the two.

C. Only a FortiAnalyzer device can send the alert notification in the form of a syslog message.

D. Both the FortiGate and FortiAnalyzer devices can send alert notifications in the form of an email alert.

QUESTION 131

Which of the following report templates must be used when scheduling report generation?

A. Layout Template
B. Data Filter Template
C. Output Template
D. Chart Template

QUESTION 132

In which of the following report templates would you configure the charts to be included in the report?

A. Layout Template
B. Data Filter Template
C. Output Template
D. Schedule Template

QUESTION 133

An administrator wishes to generate a report showing Top Traffic by service type. They notice that web traffic overwhelms the pie chart and want to exclude the web traffic from the report. Which of the following statements best describes how to do this?

A. In the Service field of the Data Filter, type 80/tcp and select the NOT checkbox.

B. Add the following entry to the Generic Field section of the Data Filter: service="!web".

C. When editing the chart, uncheck wlog to indicate that Web Filtering data is being excluded when generating the chart.

D. When editing the chart, enter 'http' in the Exclude Service field.

QUESTION 134

An administrator wishes to generate a report showing Top Traffic by service type, but wants to exclude SMTP traffic from the report. Which of the following statements best describes how to do this?

A. In the Service field of the Data Filter, type 25/smtp and select the NOT checkbox.

B. Add the following entry to the Generic Field section of the Data Filter: service="!smtp".

C. When editing the chart, uncheck mlog to indicate that Mail Filtering data is being excluded when generating the chart.

D. When editing the chart, enter 'dns' in the Exclude Service field.

QUESTION 135

A portion of the device listing for a FortiAnalyzer unit is displayed in the exhibit.

Which of the following statements best describes the reason why the FortiGate 60B unit is unable to archive data to the FortiAnalyzer unit?

A. The FortiGate unit is considered an unregistered device.
B. The FortiGate unit has been blocked from sending archive data to the FortiAnalyzer device by the administrator.
C. The FortiGate unit has insufficient privileges. The administrator should edit the device entry in the FortiAnalyzer and modify the privileges.
D. The FortiGate unit is being treated as a syslog device and is only permitted to send log data.

QUESTION 136

In order to load-share traffic using multiple static routes, the routes must be configured with ...

A. the same distance and same priority.
B. the same distance and the same weight.
C. the same distance but each of them must be assigned a unique priority.
D. a distance equal to its desired weight for ECMP but all must have the same priority.

QUESTION 137

A static route is configured for a FortiGate unit from the CLI using the following commands:
config router static edit 1
set device "wan1" set distance 20
set gateway 192.168.100.1 next
end
Which of the following conditions is NOT required for this static default route to be displayed in the FortiGate unit's routing table?

A. The Administrative Status of the wan1 interface is displayed as Up.
B. The Link Status of the wan1 interface is displayed as Up.
C. All other default routes should have an equal or higher distance.
D. You must disable DHCP client on that interface.

QUESTION 138

If Routing Information Protocol (RIP) version 1 or version 2 has already been configured on a FortiGate unit, which of the following statements is correct if the routes learned through RIP need to be advertised into Open Shortest Path First (OSPF)?

A. The FortiGate unit will automatically announce all routes learned through RIP v1 or v2 to its OSPF neighbors.
B. The FortiGate unit will automatically announce all routes learned onlythrough RIP v2 to its OSPF neighbors.
C. At a minimum, the network administrator needs to enable Redistribute RIP in the OSPF Advanced Options.
D. The network administrator needs to configure a RIP to OSPF announce policy as part of the RIP settings.
E. At a minimum, the network administrator needs to enable Redistribute Default in the OSPF Advanced Options.

QUESTION 139

If Open Shortest Path First (OSPF) has already been configured on a FortiGate unit, which of the following statements is correct if the routes learned through OSPF need to be announced by Border Gateway Protocol (BGP)?

A. The FortiGate unit will automatically announce all routes learned through OSPF to its BGP peers if the FortiGate unit is configured as an OSPF Autonomous System Boundary Router (ASBR).
B. The FortiGate unit will automatically announce all routes learned through OSPF to its BGP peers if the FortiGate unit is configured as an OSPF Area Border Router (ABR).
C. At a minimum, the network administrator needs to enable Redistribute OSPF in the BGP settings.
D. The BGP local AS number must be the same as the OSPF area number of the routes learned that need to be redistributed into BGP.
E. By design, BGP cannot redistribute routes learned through OSPF.

QUESTION 140

An administrator has formed a High Availability cluster involving two FortiGate 310B units.
[Multiple upstream Layer 2 switches] -- [FortiGate HA Cluster] -- [Multiple downstream Layer 2 switches]
The administrator wishes to ensure that a single link failure will have minimal impact upon the overall throughput of traffic through this cluster. Which of the following options describes the best step the administrator can take?
The administrator should...

A. set up a full-mesh design which uses redundant interfaces.
B. increase the number of FortiGate units in the cluster and configure HA in Active-Active mode.
C. enable monitoring of all active interfaces.
D. configure the HA ping server feature to allow for HA failover in the event that a path is disrupted.

QUESTION 141

In a High Availability configuration operating in Active-Active mode, which of the following correctly describes the path taken by a load-balanced HTTP session?

A. Request: Internal Host -> Master FG -> Slave FG -> Internet -> Web Server
B. Request: Internal Host -> Master FG -> Slave FG -> Master FG -> Internet -> Web Server
C. Request: Internal Host -> Slave FG -> Internet -> Web Server
D. Request: Internal Host -> Slave FG -> Master FG -> Internet -> Web Server

QUESTION 142

Which of the following statements is not correct regarding virtual domains (VDOMs)?

A. VDOMs divide a single FortiGate unit into two or more virtual units that function as multiple, independent units.
B. A management VDOM handles SNMP, logging, alert email, and FDN-based updates.
C. A backup management VDOM will synchronize the configuration from an active management VDOM.
D. VDOMs share firmware versions, as well as antivirus and IPS databases.
E. Only administrative users with a super_admin profile will be able to enter all VDOMs to make configuration changes.

QUESTION 143

A FortiGate unit is configured with three Virtual Domains (VDOMs) as illustrated in the exhibit.

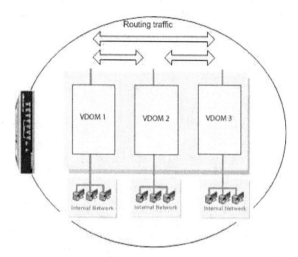

Which of the following statements are true if the network administrator wants to route traffic between all the VDOMs? (Select all that apply.)

A. The administrator should configure inter-VDOM links to avoid using external interfaces and routers.

B. As with all FortiGate unit interfaces, firewall policies must be in place for traffic to be allowed to pass through any interface, including inter-VDOM links. This provides the same level of security internally as externally.

C. This configuration requires the use of an external router.

D. Inter-VDOM routing is automatically provided if all the subnets that need to be routed are locally attached.

E. As each VDOM has an independant routing table, routing rules need to be set (for example, static routing, OSPF) in each VDOM to route traffic between VDOMs.

QUESTION 144

A FortiGate unit is configured with three Virtual Domains (VDOMs) as illustrated in the exhibit.

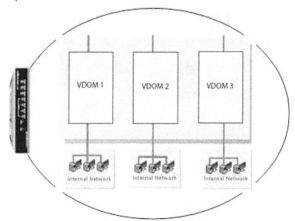

Which of the following statements are correct regarding these VDOMs? (Select all that apply.)

A. The FortiGate unit supports any combination of these VDOMs in NAT/Route and Transparent modes.
B. The FortiGate unit must be a model 1000 or above to support multiple VDOMs.
C. A license had to be purchased and applied to the FortiGate unit before VDOM mode could be enabled.
D. All VDOMs must operate in the same mode.
E. Changing a VDOM operational mode requires a reboot of the FortiGate unit.
F. An admin account can be assigned to one VDOM or it can have access to all three VDOMs.

QUESTION 145

A FortiGate administrator configures a Virtual Domain (VDOM) for a new customer. After creating the VDOM, the administrator is unable to reassign the dmz interface to the new VDOM as the option is greyed out in Web Config in the management VDOM.

What would be a possible cause for this problem?

A. The dmz interface is referenced in the configuration of another VDOM.
B. The administrator does not have the proper permissions to reassign the dmz interface.
C. Non-management VDOMs can not reference physical interfaces.
D. The dmz interface is in PPPoE or DHCP mode.
E. Reassigning an interface to a different VDOM can only be done through the CLI.

QUESTION 146

A FortiGate unit is operating in NAT/Route mode and is configured with two Virtual LAN (VLAN) sub-interfaces added to the same physical interface. Which of the following statements is correct regarding the VLAN IDs in this scenario?

A. The two VLAN sub-interfaces can have the same VLAN ID only if they have IP addresses in different subnets.
B. The two VLAN sub-interfaces must have different VLAN IDs.
C. The two VLAN sub-interfaces can have the same VLAN ID only if they belong to different VDOMs.
D. The two VLAN sub-interfaces can have the same VLAN ID if they are connected to different L2 IEEE 802.1Q compliant switches.

QUESTION 147

An intermittent connectivity issue is noticed between two devices located behind the FortiGate dmz and internal interfaces. A continuous sniffer trace is run on the FortiGate unit that the administrator will convert into a .cap file for an off-line analysis with a sniffer application.

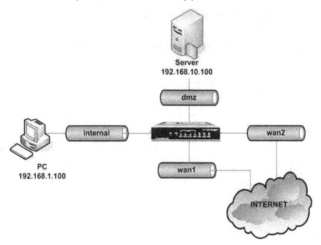

Given the high volume of global traffic on the network, which of the following CLI commands will best allow the administrator to perform this troubleshooting operation?

A. diagnose sniffer packet any
B. diagnose sniffer packet dmz "" 3
C. diagnose sniffer packet any "host 192.168.1.100 and host 192.168.10.100 " 3
D. diagnose sniffer packet any "host 192.168.1.100 and host 192.168.10.100 " 4

QUESTION 148

The Host Check feature can be enabled on the FortiGate unit
for SSL VPN connections. When this feature is enabled, the
FortiGate unit probes the remote host computer to verify that it
is "safe" before access is granted.
Which of the following items is NOT an option as part of the
Host Check feature?

A. FortiClient Antivirus software
B. Microsoft Windows Firewall software
C. FortiClient Firewall software
D. Third-party Antivirus software

QUESTION 149

In the Tunnel Mode widget of the web portal, the administrator
has configured an IP Pool and enabled split tunneling. Which of
the following statements is true about the IP address used by
the SSL VPN client?

A. The IP pool specified in the SSL-VPN Tunnel Mode Widget
   Options will override the IP address range defined in the
   SSL-VPN Settings.
B. Because split tunneling is enabled, no IP address needs to
   be assigned for the SSL VPN tunnel to be established.
C. The IP address range specified in SSL-VPN Settings will
   override the IP address range in the SSL-VPN Tunnel Mode
   Widget Options.

QUESTION 150

An issue could potentially occur when clicking Connect to start tunnel mode SSL VPN. The tunnel will start up for a few seconds, then shut down. Which of the following statements best describes how to resolve this issue?

A. This user does not have permission to enable tunnel mode. Make sure that the tunnel mode widget has been added to that user's web portal.
B. This FortiGate unit may have multiple Internet connections. To avoid this problem, use the appropriate CLI command to bind the SSL VPN connection to the original incoming interface.
C. Check the SSL adaptor on the host machine. If necessary, uninstall and reinstall the adaptor from the tunnel mode portal.
D. Make sure that only Internet Explorer is used. All other browsers are unsupported.

QUESTION 151

You are the administrator in charge of a FortiGate unit which acts as a VPN gateway. You have chosen to use Interface Mode when configuring the VPN tunnel and you want users from either side to be able to initiate new sessions. There is only 1 subnet at either end and the FortiGate unit already has a default route.
Which of the following configuration steps are required to achieve these objectives? (Select all that apply.)

A. Create one firewall policy.
B. Create two firewall policies.
C. Add a route for the remote subnet.
D. Add a route for incoming traffic.
E. Create a phase 1 definition.
F. Create a phase 2 definition.

QUESTION 152

A network administrator needs to implement dynamic route redundancy between a FortiGate unit located in a remote office and a FortiGate unit located in the central office.
The remote office accesses central resources using IPSec VPN tunnels through two different Internet providers.
What is the best method for allowing the remote office access to the resources through the FortiGate unit used at the central office?

A. Use two or more route-based IPSec VPN tunnels and enable OSPF on the IPSec virtual interfaces.
B. Use two or more policy-based IPSec VPN tunnels and enable OSPF on the IPSec virtual interfaces.
C. Use route-based VPNs on the central office FortiGate unit to advertise routes with a dynamic routing protocol and use a policy-based VPN on the remote office with two or more static default routes.
D. Dynamic routing protocols cannot be used over IPSec VPN tunnels.

QUESTION 153

A FortiClient fails to establish a VPN tunnel with a FortiGate unit. The following information is displayed in the FortiGate unit logs:
msg="Initiator: sent 192.168.11.101 main mode message #1 (OK)" msg="Initiator: sent 192.168.11.101 main mode message #2 (OK)" msg="Initiator: sent 192.168.11.101 main mode message #3 (OK)" msg="Initiator: parsed 192.168.11.101 main mode message #3 (DONE)" msg="Initiator: sent 192.168.11.101 quick mode message #1 (OK)" msg="Initiator: tunnel 192.168.1.1/192.168.11.101 install ipsec sa" msg="Initiator: sent 192.168.11.101 quick mode message #2 (DONE)" msg="Initiator: tunnel 192.168.11.101, transform=ESP_3DES, HMAC_MD5" msg="Failed to acquire an IP address
Which of the following statements is a possible cause for the failure to establish the VPN tunnel?

A. An IPSec DHCP server is not enabled on the external interface of the FortiGate unit.
B. There is no IPSec firewall policy configured for the policy-based VPN.
C. There is a mismatch between the FortiGate unit and the FortiClient IP addresses in the phase 2 settings.
D. The phase 1 configuration on the FortiGate unit uses Aggressive mode while FortiClient uses Main mode.

QUESTION 154

An administrator sets up a new FTP server on TCP port 2121.
A FortiGate unit is located between the FTP clients and the
server. The administrator has created a policy for TCP port
2121.
Users have been complaining that when downloading data they
receive a 200 Port command successful message followed by a
425 Cannot build data connection message.
Which of the following statements represents the best solution
to this problem?

A. Create a new session helper for the FTP service monitoring
port 2121.

B. Enable the ANY service in the firewall policies for both
incoming and outgoing traffic.

C. Place the client and server interface in the same zone and
enable intra-zone traffic.

D. Disable any protection profiles being applied to FTP traffic.

QUESTION 155

Which of the following Session TTL values will take
precedence?

A. Session TTL specified at the system level for that port
number

B. Session TTL specified in the matching firewall policy

C. Session TTL dictated by the application control list
associated with the matching firewall policy

D. The default session TTL specified at the system level

QUESTION 156

Which of the following items is NOT a packet characteristic matched by a firewall service object?

A. ICMP type and code
B. TCP/UDP source and destination ports
C. IP protocol number
D. TCP sequence number

QUESTION 157

A network administrator connects his PC to the INTERNAL interface on a FortiGate unit. The administrator attempts to make an HTTPS connection to the FortiGate unit on the VLAN1 interface at the IP address of 10.0.1.1, but gets no connectivity. The following troubleshooting commands are executed from the DOS prompt on the PC and from the CLI. C:\>ping 10.0.1.1
Pinging 10.0.1.1 with 32 bytes of data:
Reply from 10.0.1.1: bytes=32 time=1ms TTL=255 Reply from 10.0.1.1: bytes=32 time<1ms TTL=255 Reply from 10.0.1.1: bytes=32 time<1ms TTL=255 Reply from 10.0.1.1: bytes=32 time<1ms TTL=255 user1 # get system interface
== [internal]
namE. internal modE. static ip: 10.0.1.254 255.255.255.128 status: up netbios-forwarD. disable typE. physical mtu-overridE. disable
== [vlan1]
namE. vlan1 modE. static ip: 10.0.1.1 255.255.255.128 status: up netb ios-forwarD. disable typE. vlan mtu-overridE. disable user1 # diagnose debug flow trace start 100 user1 # diagnose debug ena
user1 # diagnose debug flow filter daddr 10.0.1.1 10.0.1.1
id=20085 trace_id=274 msg="vd-root received a packet(proto=6, 10.0.1.130:47927->10.0.1.1:443) from internal." id=20085 trace_id=274 msg="allocate a new session-00000b1b"
id=20085 trace_id=274 msg="find SNAT: IP-10.0.1.1, port-43798" id=20085 trace_id=274 msg="iprope_in_check() check failed, drop"
Based on the output from these commands, which of the following explanations is a possible cause of the problem?

A. The Fortigate unit has no route back to the PC.
B. The PC has an IP address in the wrong subnet.
C. The PC is using an incorrect default gateway IP address.
D. The FortiGate unit does not have the HTTPS service configured on the VLAN1 interface.
E. There is no firewall policy allowing traffic from INTERNAL-> VLAN1.

QUESTION 158

A network administrator connects his PC to the INTERNAL interface on a FortiGate unit. The administrator attempts to make an HTTPS connection to the FortiGate unit on the VLAN1 interface at the IP address of 10.0.1.1, but gets no connectivity. The following troubleshooting commands are executed from the CLI:
user1 # get system interface
== [internal]
namE. internal modE. static ip: 10.0.1.254 255.255.255.128 status: up netbios-forwarD. disable typE. physical mtu-overridE. disable
== [vlan1]
namE. vlan1 modE. static ip: 10.0.1.1 255.255.255.128 status: up netb ios-forwarD. disable typE. vlan mtu-overridE. disable
user1 # get router info routing-table all
Codes: K - kernel, C - connected, S - static, R - RIP, B - BGP O - OSPF, IA - OSPF inter area
N1 - OSPF NSSA external type 1, N2 - OSPF NSSA external type 2 E1 - OSPF external type 1, E2 - OSPF external type 2
i - IS-IS, L1 - IS-IS level-1, L2 - IS-IS level-2, ia - IS-IS inter area
* - candidate default
S 10.0.0.0/8 [10/0] is a summary, Null
C 10.0.1.0/25 is directly connected, vlan1
C 10.0.1.128/25 is directly connected, internal user1 # diagnose debug flow trace start 100 user1 # diagnose debug ena
user1 # diagnose debug flow filter daddr 10.0.1.1 10.0.1.1
id=20085 trace_id=277 msg="vd-root received a packet(proto=6, 10.0.1.130
:47922->10.0.1.1:443) from internal."
id=20085 trace_id=277 msg="allocate a new session-

00000b21" id=20085 trace_id=277 msg="iprope_in_check()
check failed, drop"
Based on the output from these commands, which of the
following is a possible cause of the problem?

A. The FortiGate unit has no route back to the PC.
B. The PC has an IP address in the wrong subnet.
C. The PC is using an incorrect default gateway IP address.
D. There is no firewall policy allowing traffic from INTERNAL ->
   VLAN1.

QUESTION 159

WAN optimization is configured in Active/Passive mode. When
will the remote peer accept an attempt to initiate a tunnel?

A. The attempt will be accepted when the request comes from
   a known peer and there is a matching WAN optimization
   passive rule.
B. The attempt will be accepted when there is a matching
   WAN optimization passive rule.
C. The attempt will be accepted when the request comes from
   a known peer.
D. The attempt will be accepted when a user on the remote
   peer accepts the connection request.

QUESTION 160

Which of the following methods does the FortiGate unit use to
determine the availability of a web cache using Web Cache
Communication Protocol (WCCP)?

A. The FortiGate unit receives periodic "Here I am" messages
   from the web cache.
B. The FortiGate unit polls all globally-defined web cache
   servers at a regular intervals.

C. The FortiGate using uses the health check monitor to verify the availability of a web cache server.
D. The web cache sends an "I see you" message which is captured by the FortiGate unit.

QUESTION 161

What remote authentication servers can you configure to validate your FortiAnalyzer administrator logons? (Choose three.)

A. RADIUS
B. Local
C. LDAP
D. PKI
E. TACACS+

QUESTION 162

Which two statements are correct regarding synchronization between primary and secondary devices in a FortiManager HA cluster? (Choose two.)

A. All device configurations including global databases are synchronized in the HA cluster.
B. FortiGuard databases are downloaded separately by each cluster device.
C. FortiGuard databases are downloaded by the primary FortiManager device and then synchronized with all secondary devices.
D. Local logs and log configuration settings are synchronized in the HA cluster.

QUESTION 163

Workflow mode includes which new permissions for Super_Admin administrative users?

A. Self-approval, Approval, Reject
B. Self-disapproval, Approval, Accept
C. Approval, Self-approval, Change Notification
D. Change Notification, Self-disapproval, Submit

QUESTION 164

Which two statements are correct regarding header and footer policies? (Choose two.)

A. Header and footer policies can only be created in the root ADOM.
B. Header and footer policies can only be created in the global ADOM.
C. Header and footer policies are created in policy packages and assigned to ADOM policy packages.
D. Header and footer policies can be modified in the assigned ADOM policy package.

QUESTION 165

What two statements are correct regarding administrative users and accounts? (Choose two.)

A. Administrative user accounts can exist locally or remotely.
B. Administrative user login information is available to all administrators through the Web-based manager.
C. Administrative users must be assigned an administrative profile.
D. Administrative user access is restricted by administrative profiles only.

QUESTION 166

What is the purpose of locking an ADOM revision?

A. To prevent further changes from Device Manager.
B. To disable revision history.
C. To prevent auto deletion.
D. To lock the Policy and Objects tab.

QUESTION 167

Which two statements describe a "modified" device settings' status in the Configuration and Installation Status widget of a managed FortiGate device? (Choose two.)

A. Configuration changes were made directly on the managed device.
B. Configuration changes were made from Device Manager for a managed FortiGate device.
C. Configuration changes were installed to a managed FortiGate device.
D. Configuration changes in Device Manager no longer match the latest revision in the device's revision history.

QUESTION 168

What effect do administrative domains (ADOM) have on report settings? (Choose two.)

A. None. ADOMs cannot be used with reports.
B. Reports must be configured within their own ADOM.
C. Chart Library, Macro Library, Dataset Library, and Output Profile become ADOM-specific.
D. Dataset Library becomes global for all ADOMs.

QUESTION 169

What statements are true regarding disk log quota? (Choose two.)

A. The FortiAnalyzer stops logging once the disk log quota is met.
B. The FortiAnalyzer automatically sets the disk log quota based on the device.
C. The FortiAnalyzer can overwrite the oldest logs or stop logging once the disk log quota is met.
D. The FortiAnalyzer disk quota is configurable, but has a minimum of 100MB and a maximum based on the reserved system space.

QUESTION 170

Which ports are commonly used by FortiManager? (Choose two.)

A. TCP 541 for remote management of a FortiGate unit.
B. TCP 5199 HA heartbeat or synchronization (FortiManager HA cluster).
C. TCP 703 HA heartbeat or synchronization (FortiManager HA cluster).
D. TCP 514 for remote management of a FortiGate unit.

QUESTION 171

What statements are true regarding FortiAnalyzer's treatment of high availability (HA) clusters? (Choose two.)

A. FortiAnalyzer distinguishes different devices by their serial number.
B. FortiAnalyzer receives logs from all devices in a cluster.
C. FortiAnalyzer receives logs only from the primary device in the cluster.
D. FortiAnalyzer only needs to know the serial number of the primary device in the cluster—it automatically discovers the other devices.

QUESTION 172

Refer to the exhibit. What does the clock icon denote beside the Bandwidth and Applications Report?

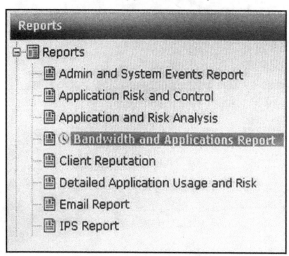

A. It is a custom report.
B. It is an imported report from either a different FortiAnalyzer device or a different (but supported) ADOM.
C. It is in the process of generating.
D. It is a scheduled report.

QUESTION 173

What statements are true regarding Administrative Domains (ADOMs)? (Choose three.)

A. ADOMs are a way to group devices for administrators to monitor and manage.
B. Administrators with the standard_user administrator profile can view all ADOMs.
C. The Web-based navigation changes when ADOMs are enabled.
D. The admin administrator can assign one device to multiple ADOMs.
E. The admin administrator can assign more than one ADOMs to a single administrator.

QUESTION 174

What is the primary difference between raw format logs and formatted format logs?

A. Raw logs can be viewed in the CLI only.
B. Raw logs display logs as they appear within the log file.
C. Raw logs are more human-consumable than formatted format logs.
D. Raw logs cannot be downloaded into .csv format.

QUESTION 175

Which two statements are correct regarding the "Import all Objects" setting in the import policy wizard? (Choose two.)

A. All used and unused objects will be imported into the ADOM object database.
B. Only used objects will be imported into the ADOM object database.
C. FortiManager allows only policy dependent objects to be imported into an ADOM object database.
D. Any unused object on the FortiGate device will be deleted with the first policy install from FortiManager.

QUESTION 176

Which statement is true regarding FortiAnalyzer models?

A. All physical appliances can support the same number of GB per day of logs.
B. Both physical and virtual appliances have same license file.
C. All physical appliances have the same storage capacity.
D. The virtual appliance license determines the number of devices supported and the amount of traffic can be collected.

QUESTION 177

Which statement is true regarding the import/export feature?

A. This is only a feature for reports.
B. This feature is for reports and charts.
C. This feature is for reports, charts, and datasets.
D. This feature is for reports and datasets.

QUESTION 178

Refer to the exhibit. Examine the logs from the FortiView > Log View page:

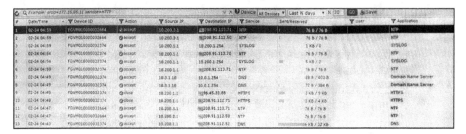

What is one possible reason this search result yields no results?

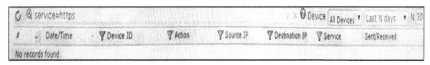

A. You cannot use SQL syntax in the Search field of the FortiView > Log View page.
B. Case Sensitive Search is enabled.
C. There are no logs that include https as a service.
D. You cannot search for logs from the FortiView > Log View page.

QUESTION 179

What is the problem with the following SQL SELECT statement?

```
SELECT dstip as "Destination IP", count(*) as session FROM
$log-traffic GROUP BY dstip WHERE $filter and dstip is not null
```

A. The clauses are not coded in the right sequence.
B. $log-traffic is not a log type.
C. The FROM clause is not required.
D. SQL queries are case-sensitive.

QUESTION 180

What statements are true regarding RAID? (Choose three.)

A. RAID is supported on all FortiAnalyzer models (both hardware appliances and virtual appliances).
B. RAID backs up log information.
C. RAID requires multiple identical drives.
D. RAID levels determine how data is distributed across drives.
E. RAID status is available via the CLI only.

QUESTION 181

How does the Log View page display logs when ADOMs are enabled?

A. The Log View page displays logs in ADOMs together so they appear as a single device.
B. The Log View page displays logs per ADOM.
C. The Log View page cannot display raw logs when ADOMs are enabled.
D. The Log View page cannot display logs in real-time when ADOMs are enabled.

QUESTION 182

Refer to the exhibit. An administrator created a new interface object named Dev and configured dynamic mapping for the wan2 interface on the HeadOffice FortiGate. A new policy from internal to Dev is configured. Which statement is correct regarding the installation of the HeadOffice policy package?

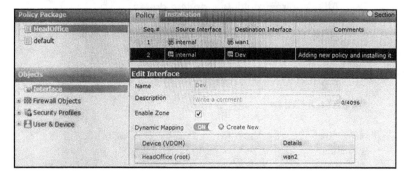

A. A new zone named Dev with member interface wan2 and a policy from internal to Dev will be created on the FortiGate device.

B. A new policy from internal to wan2 will be created locally on the FortiGate.

C. Dev is a FortiManager reference for interface wan2 on the HeadOffice FortiGate. No zone is created on the FortiGate.

D. The install will fail because wan2 cannot be mapped to Dev. This is not a valid configuration.

QUESTION 183

On the Device Manager tab, what does a red circle in the Logs field of a device indicate?

A. A red circle indicates logs are being received.

B. A red circle indicates the IPSec tunnel is down.

C. A red circle indicates logs are not being received.

D. A red circle indicates no recent logs have been received.

QUESTION 184

A user creates a policy package with two installation targets, as shown in the exhibit. When the install operation is performed, which two statements are correct concerning the Install On column in the policy configuration? (Choose two.)

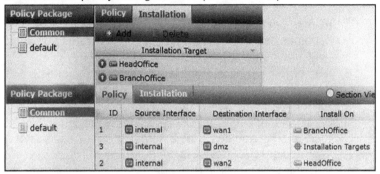

A. Policy ID 3 will not be installed on any FortiGate device.
B. Policy ID 3 will be installed on both FortiGate devices.
C. Policy ID 2 will be installed only on the HeadOffice FortiGate device.
D. Install On column values represent successful installations.

QUESTION 185

Which two statements are correct regarding FortiGuard features on FortiManager? (Choose two.)

A. FortiManager can function as a local FortiGuard Distribution Server (FDS).
B. In FortiManager HA only master FortiManager can act as an FDS server.
C. When FortiManager is configured for closed network operation, it can connect to public FDS servers to obtain managed device information and sync packages.
D. FortiGuard information is not synchronized across a FortiManager cluster

QUESTION 186

When configuring FortiGuard on FortiManager, which two statements are correct regarding Allow Push Update settings configured in the FortiGuard Antivirus and IPS Settings? (Choose two.)

A. If an urgent or critical FortiGuard Antivirus and/or IPS update becomes available, the FortiManager built-in FDS will send push update notifications to each managed device.
B. If an urgent or critical FortiGuard Antivirus and/or IPS update becomes available, the FortiManager built-in FDS will receive push update notifications.
C. FortiManager's built-in FDS service may not correctly receive push updates if the external facing IP address of any intermediary NAT device is dynamic.
D. FortiManager's built-in FDS service does not allow an administrator to override the default FortiManager IP address and port used by the FDN to send update messages.

QUESTION 187

Which of the following methods is best suited to changing device level settings on existing and future managed FortiGate devices?

A. Configure each managed FortiGate device and install.
B. Configure using provisioning templates and install.
C. Configure using CLI-only objects and install.
D. Configure a script for these settings and install.

QUESTION 188

FortiAnalyzer centralizes which functions? (Choose three.)

A. Network analysis
B. Graphical reporting
C. Content archiving / data mining
D. Vulnerability assessment
E. Security log analysis / forensics

QUESTION 189
Setting workspace-mode to normal, as shown in the exhibit, allows what on FortiManager? (Choose two.)

```
config system global
set workspace-mode normal end
```

A. ADOM locking
B. VDOM locking
C. Unrestricted concurrent access
D. Restricted concurrent access

QUESTION 190

A user selects Install Config for a managed FortiGate device, as shown in the exhibit.

Which two statements are true regarding this action? (Choose two.)

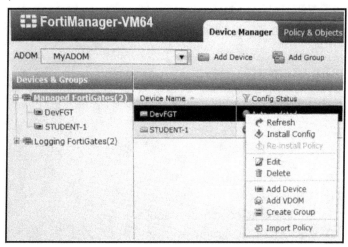

A. It provides the option to preview configuration changes prior to installing them.

B. It allows you to perform a quick install of device level settings, without the need to launch the Install wizard.

C. Once initiated, the install process cannot be cancelled and changes will be installed on the managed device.

D. It will launch the Install wizard to install any configuration changes to the managed device.

ANSWERS

1. Correct Answer: C
2. Correct Answer: AC
3. Correct Answer: B
4. Correct Answer: ABCDE
5. Correct Answer: C
6. Correct Answer: A
7. Correct Answer: ABC
8. Correct Answer: A
9. Correct Answer: B
10. Correct Answer: ABC
11. Correct Answer: A
12. Correct Answer: A
13. Correct Answer: BCD
14. Correct Answer: D
15. Correct Answer: D
16. Correct Answer: A
17. Correct Answer: A
18. Correct Answer: B
19. Correct Answer: ABC
20. Correct Answer: ABCD
21. Correct Answer: D
22. Correct Answer: A
23. Correct Answer: B
24. Correct Answer: ABC
25. Correct Answer: ABC
26. Correct Answer: B
27. Correct Answer: BCD
28. Correct Answer: A
29. Correct Answer: A
30. Correct Answer: ABC
31. Correct Answer: ABC
32. Correct Answer: AB
33. Correct Answer: AD
34. Correct Answer: B
35. Correct Answer: B

36. Correct Answer: BCEF
37. Correct Answer: D
38. Correct Answer: A
39. Correct Answer: A
40. Correct Answer: A
41. Correct Answer: BCD
42. Correct Answer: AB
43. Correct Answer: BCD
44. Correct Answer: A
45. Correct Answer: BE
46. Correct Answer: ABCD
47. Correct Answer: BE
48. Correct Answer: ABCE
49. Correct Answer: A
50. Correct Answer: ABCD
51. Correct Answer: C
52. Correct Answer: ABC
53. Correct Answer: ABC
54. Correct Answer: C
55. Correct Answer: D
56. Correct Answer: A
57. Correct Answer: B
58. Correct Answer: A
59. Correct Answer: B
60. Correct Answer: A
61. Correct Answer: A
62. Correct Answer: A
63. Correct Answer: A
64. Correct Answer: B
65. Correct Answer: B
66. Correct Answer: A
67. Correct Answer: AE
68. Correct Answer: D
69. Correct Answer: A
70. Correct Answer: ABC
71. Correct Answer: BCD
72. Correct Answer: C
73. Correct Answer: B
74. Correct Answer: ABC
75. Correct Answer: ABD

76. Correct Answer: BC
77. Correct Answer: AB
78. Correct Answer: C
79. Correct Answer: CDE
80. Correct Answer: A
81. Correct Answer: BD
82. Correct Answer: B
83. Correct Answer: A
84. Correct Answer: ABC
85. Correct Answer: BD
86. Correct Answer: CDE
87. Correct Answer: AC
88. Correct Answer: A
89. Correct Answer: A
90. Correct Answer: BE
91. Correct Answer: A
92. Correct Answer: C
93. Correct Answer: AC
94. Correct Answer: AD
95. Correct Answer: AD
96. Correct Answer: AD
97. Correct Answer: AD
98. Correct Answer: AB
99. Correct Answer: B
100. Correct Answer: BD
101. Correct Answer: B
102. Correct Answer: BE
103. Correct Answer: BC
104. Correct Answer: AC
105. Correct Answer: AB
106. Correct Answer: AB
107. Correct Answer: C
108. Correct Answer: C
109. Correct Answer: A
110. Correct Answer: AB
111. Correct Answer: B
112. Correct Answer: C
113. Correct Answer: B
114. Correct Answer: AC
115. Correct Answer: B

116.	Correct Answer: C
117.	Correct Answer: AC
118.	Correct Answer: C
119.	Correct Answer: A
120.	Correct Answer: A
121.	Correct Answer: ABD
122.	Correct Answer: A
123.	Correct Answer: A
124.	Correct Answer: A
125.	Correct Answer: A
126.	Correct Answer: A
127.	Correct Answer: AB
128.	Correct Answer: A
129.	Correct Answer: A
130.	Correct Answer: A
131.	Correct Answer: A
132.	Correct Answer: A
133.	Correct Answer: A
134.	Correct Answer: A
135.	Correct Answer: A
136.	Correct Answer: A
137.	Correct Answer: D
138.	Correct Answer: C
139.	Correct Answer: C
140.	Correct Answer: A
141.	Correct Answer: A
142.	Correct Answer: A
143.	Correct Answer: ABE
144.	Correct Answer: AF
145.	Correct Answer: A
146.	Correct Answer: B
147.	Correct Answer: C
148.	Correct Answer: B
149.	Correct Answer: A
150.	Correct Answer: B
151.	Correct Answer: BCEF
152.	Correct Answer: A
153.	Correct Answer: A
154.	Correct Answer: A
155.	Correct Answer: C

156.	Correct Answer: D
157.	Correct Answer: D
158.	Correct Answer: D
159.	Correct Answer: A
160.	Correct Answer: C
161.	Correct Answer: ABC
162.	Correct Answer: AB
163.	Correct Answer: C
164.	Correct Answer: BC
165.	Correct Answer: AC
166.	Correct Answer: A
167.	Correct Answer: AB
168.	Correct Answer: BC
169.	Correct Answer: CD
170.	Correct Answer: AB
171.	Correct Answer: AC
172.	Correct Answer: D
173.	Correct Answer: ACE
174.	Correct Answer: B
175.	Correct Answer: AD
176.	Correct Answer: D
177.	Correct Answer: B
178.	Correct Answer: B
179.	Correct Answer: A

Explanation:

GROUP BY must come after the WHERE statement.

180.	Correct Answer: CDE
181.	Correct Answer: B
182.	Correct Answer: C
183.	Correct Answer: D
184.	Correct Answer: AC
185.	Correct Answer:AB
186.	Correct Answer: BC
187.	Correct Answer: B
188.	Correct Answer: BCE
189.	Correct Answer: AD

References:

http://docs.fortinet.com/uploaded/files/2250/FortiManag er-5.2.1-Administration-Guide.pdf

190. **Correct Answer: BC**

www.ingramcontent.com/pod-product-compliance
Lightning Source LLC
LaVergne TN
LVHW051707050326
832903LV00032B/4062